DOCTOR-ASSISTED SUICIDE

and the Euthanasia Movement

Revised Edition!

IDEAS in CONFLICT

Gary E. McCuen

GEM

GARY McCUEN

publications inc.

411 Mallalieu Drive
Hudson, Wisconsin 54016
Phone (715) 386-7113

Illustration and Photo Credits

Chan Lowe 125; Craig MacIntosh 12; Eleanor Mill 107; David Seavey 27, 94; Bill Schorr 63; Mike Smith 131; Wayne Stayskal 90; Richard Wright 58, 142.

GEM
GARY McCUEN
publications inc.

© 1999 by Gary E. McCuen Publications, Inc.
411 Mallalieu Drive, Hudson, Wisconsin 54016

(715) 386-7113

International Standard Book Number
0-86596-178-6
Printed in the United States of America

CONTENTS

Ideas in Conflict

Chapter 1   EUTHANASIA IN PRACTICE: THE CASE OF THE NETHERLANDS

Chapter 2   THE OREGON LAW

REASONING SKILL DEVELOPMENT
These activities may be used as individualized study guides for students in libraries and resource centers or as discussion catalysts in small group and classroom discussions.

IDEAS
in CONFLICT

This series features ideas in conflict on political, social, and moral issues. It presents counterpoints, debates, opinions, commentary, and analysis for use in libraries and classrooms. Each title in the series uses one or more of the following basic elements:

Introductions *that present an issue overview giving historic background and/or a description of the controversy.*

Counterpoints *and debates carefully chosen from publications, books, and position papers on the political right and left to help librarians and teachers respond to requests that treatment of public issues be fair and balanced.*

Symposiums *and forums that go beyond debates that can polarize and oversimplify. These present commentary from across the political spectrum that reflect how complex issues attract many shades of opinion.*

A **global** *emphasis with foreign perspectives and surveys on various moral questions and political issues that will help readers to place subject matter in a less culture-bound and ethnocentric frame of reference. In an ever-shrinking and interdependent world, understanding and cooperation are essential. Many issues are global in nature and can be effectively dealt with only by common efforts and international understanding.*

Reasoning skill *study guides and discussion activities provide ready-made tools for helping with critical reading and evaluation of content. The guides and activities deal with one or more of the following:*

RECOGNIZING AUTHOR'S POINT OF VIEW

INTERPRETING EDITORIAL CARTOONS

VALUES IN CONFLICT

COMPARING CULTURAL VALUES

IN MY OPINION

WHAT IS EDITORIAL BIAS?

WHAT IS SEX BIAS?

WHAT IS POLITICAL BIAS?

WHAT IS ETHNOCENTRIC BIAS?

WHAT IS RACE BIAS?

WHAT IS RELIGIOUS BIAS?

*From across **the political spectrum** varied sources are presented for research projects and classroom discussions. Diverse opinions in the series come from magazines, newspapers, syndicated columnists, books, political speeches, foreign nations, and position papers by corporations and nonprofit institutions.*

About the Editor

The late Gary E. McCuen was an editor and publisher of anthologies for libraries and discussion materials for schools and colleges. His publications have specialized in social, moral and political conflict. They include books, pamphlets, cassettes, tabloids, filmstrips and simulation games, most of them created from his many years of experience in teaching and educational publishing.

HISTORICAL PERSPECTIVES: PHYSICIAN AID-IN-DYING
(ACTIVE VOLUNTARY EUTHANASIA)

Edwin R. Dubose

Edwin R. DuBose wrote the following article in his capacity as contributing editor at The Park Ridge Center. The article presents historical perspectives on euthanasia, and was included in publication of the Park Ridge Center in Chicago, 676 North St. Clair, Suite 450, Chicago, Illinois 60611, published by Trinity Press International.

■ POINTS TO CONSIDER

1. Explain the Greek concept of a "good death" and "freedom to leave."

2. What early Christian beliefs about human life and suffering prohibited euthanasia?

3. How did nineteenth century medical advances bring in the age of "heroic medicine?"

4. Contrast "passive euthanasia" with "active euthanasia."

"A Brief Historical Perspective on Euthanasia," by Edwin R. Dubose from **Choosing Death: Active Euthanasia, Religion, and the Public Debate,** ed. by Ron Hamel (Valley Forge, PA: Trinity Press International, 1991) pp.15-25. Reprinted with permission.

For the Romans and the Greeks, dying decently and rationally mattered immensely.

Active voluntary euthanasia is not new to the latter part of the twentieth century. Even in ancient societies, terminally ill people requested to have their dying hastened, though the meaning of euthanasia for them differed from its meaning today. What seems new is the cultural context in which the question of euthanasia arises. Many factors contribute to this new context, but perhaps most influential are the sophistication and availability of medical technology and the social, scientific, moral, and religious beliefs that permeate modern American society....

Because the English word *euthanasia* is taken from the Greek *eu thanatos*, "good or easy death," this review begins with classical antiquity.

CLASSICAL ANTIQUITY

In the present day the term *euthanasia* is associated with the act of mercifully ending the life of a hopelessly suffering patient. The classical understanding of what is now called euthanasia, however, was broader in scope. Focusing on the act of hastening death, the contemporary question involving euthanasia tends to be: Is euthanasia under any conditions morally justifiable? For the ancients, in contrast, euthanasia did not necessarily imply an act, a means, or a method of causing or hastening death. The focus was on one possible manner of dying, and the pivotal question was: Did the person voluntarily meet death with peace of mind and minimal pain? The Greeks sometimes employed the term to describe the "spiritual" state of the dying person at the impending moment of death; it was important that the person die a "good death," in a psychologically balanced state of mind, under composed circumstances, in a condition of self-control. To ensure such a death, it was permissible to shorten a person's life.

Moreover, for the Greeks and Romans, a "good death" was not anchored in a medical context alone, nor did it carry the contemporary negative connotations of suicide. Their stress was on the voluntary and reasoned nature of the dying, and they were generally sympathetic to active voluntary euthanasia, provided that the deed was done for the right reasons, for example, to end the suffering of a terminal illness. In this sense, the English language has lost touch with many of the characteristic Greek and Roman

9

understandings of active euthanasia, which tended to emphasize it as a mode of death, a way of dying, carefully distinguished from murder or suicide.

In classical antiquity, then, there was a generally recognized, although qualified, tolerance of the "freedom to leave," which permitted the sick or suffering to terminate their lives. Furthermore, under the appropriate circumstances, it was permissible for others to administer the means of death....

THE CHRISTIAN ERA

For the Romans and the Greeks, dying decently and rationally mattered immensely. In a sense, how they died was a measure of the final value of life, especially for a life wasted by disease and suffering. For early Christians, however, this was not a consideration. Because only God had the right to give and take life, active euthanasia was viewed as an illicit exercise of a divine prerogative.

Generally, the practice of active euthanasia among the sick became unusual after about the second century A.D., because of the growing acceptance of the importance placed by Judeo-Christian teachings upon individual life and the endurance of suffering. By the fifth century, Augustine held that life and its suffering were divinely ordained by God and must be borne accordingly. A human was created in the image of God, and his or her life thus belonged to God; the time and manner of death was God's will and God's only. Moreover, as the writings of the New Testament assumed canonical form, suffering was viewed by Christians as something in which they could rejoice for two reasons: (1) God used suffering as a means of producing spiritual maturity; and (2) the very fact that Christians endured suffering was proof that they were children of God. Christians were to engage in an active, direct ministry of consolation and encouragement of their fellow sufferers. The relief to be provided was not removal of the suffering but a consolation that transformed the suffering into a positive force in the person's life. Thus the belief developed that one should not abandon the life assigned to him or her by God but should endure it in the hope of a certain resurrection. These influences helped to shape social, moral, and religious attitudes toward illness and disability and acceptance of suffering at the time of death. As the ethic of respect for human life achieved this moral status, the early Christians declared it the absolute standard of right conduct for doctor and patient alike. Finally, although Christian charity brought a heightened sense of responsibility to relieve suffering, the Biblical commandment against killing seemed to prohibit absolutely the taking of a person's life even to relieve suffering.

During the next eight centuries, views of euthanasia were shaped by moral and legal prohibitions endorsed by the authority of the Catholic church. In the thirteenth century, Thomas Aquinas argued that shortening one's life was sinful not only because it violated a commandment but because it left no time for the person's repentance. Also, taking one's own life or the life of another was against the law of nature and contrary to charity. Such an act was not lawful because every person belonged to the community, and it was a sin against God because life was a gift and subject only to God's powers. Given the Christian proscriptions against active euthanasia for any reason, the sense of a "good" death was reinterpreted: the Christian was supposed to be tranquil and accepting at death. The means by which this acceptance was to be achieved included primarily physical comfort, moral support, and prayer. This essentially passive process was largely independent of the physician; the clergy, family, and friends prepared the patient for a good, "Christian" death.

A theoretical discussion of active euthanasia was presented by Sir Thomas More in his *Utopia*, first published in 1516. In his vision of the ideal society, "if a disease is not only incurable but also distressing and agonizing without cessation, then the priests and the public officials exhort the man...to free himself from this bitter life...or else voluntarily permit others to free him." Although the English term had not yet been coined, More clearly described the active form of euthanasia. In his essay he offered no discussion of the physician's role; he did outline, however, certain precautions to be taken to avoid possible abuses of the practice.

More's comments on euthanasia are significant when viewed against the religious, social, and political climate of this general period. As gathering theological storm clouds gave way to Luther's thundering against Rome, one's understanding of Christian faith became crucially important. The reformers in the reign of Henry VIII, to whom More succumbed, and later those in Elizabeth's reign, faced a formidable task in converting the people to Protestantism. Following an Augustinian argument against

11

Illustration by Craig MacIntosh. Reprinted with permission, **Star Tribune,** Mpls.

euthanasia as an evil caused by a lack of faith, they viewed euthanasia as the antithesis of the faith that every Christian needed in order to be saved; it represented the opposite of pious hope....

THE NINETEENTH CENTURY

The role of the physician in dealing with the dying patient received significant attention in the early nineteenth century. During the previous decades, the enthusiasms of the Enlightenment faith in human progress led to the elaboration of a number of ambitious, this-worldly alternatives to Christian attitudes toward illness, suffering and death. Because of the human ability to know and control the natural, physical world, a number of Enlightenment philosophers believed that biomedical research, public health programs, and progressive thinking would result in a much extended life span. Now that science had been freed from religion's superstition and ignorance, Benjamin Franklin predicted, the new scientific and medical advances would make possible human longevity of a thousand years or more. In spite of this optimism, however, by 1800 the limits of medical achievement were recognized. Medicine, it was argued, could not conquer death, but the physician could marshal medicine's forces to slow down the tragically inevitable process of decline. As part of the effort to ward off premature death, new devices were developed to prevent pain and relieve distress, and these required the expert intervention and guidance of the medical profession and inaugurated the age of heroic medicine.

This new level of medical intervention to prolong life prompted the criticism that physicians were needlessly prolonging the dying process. A number of articles written in Europe and America during the late eighteenth and early nineteenth centuries criticized physicians who treated diseases rather than patients. Many of these pieces discussed the role of the physician in promoting the classical notion of harmonious death. After noting the tendency of physicians to neglect a patient once an illness was found to be terminal, the author of one article in 1826 urged doctors to accept responsibility for their patients' "spiritual" euthanasia. Physical and moral comfort were to be provided, but heroic medications likely to prolong the dying and extend a person's suffering were to be avoided. At the same time, the author condemned the thought of hastening a patient's death. However, medical and therapeutic advances during the century made heroic intervention increasingly possible and set the stage for open advocacy of the practice of active euthanasia....

Samuel D. Williams, schoolmaster and essayist, in 1870 published the first paper to deal entirely with the concept of active voluntary euthanasia and its application. There he advocated active euthanasia for all willing patients with incurable and painful diseases. Williams further argued that it was the duty of medical attendants, presumably physicians, to provide active euthanasia to their patients. Neither concern that pain and suffering should be nobly borne until a natural death nor the sense that one's life belonged to God entered his argument.

By the beginning of the twentieth century, the major elements in the contemporary arguments for and against the practice of active voluntary euthanasia had been articulated. The growth of scientific knowledge and technology led to a reconsideration of traditional moral views, accompanied by a decline in the importance of theology in shaping social views of suicide and euthanasia. Some physicians admitted having practiced active euthanasia, and others expressed sympathy for the practice. Other physicians, however, found no medical precedent to justify the sacrifice of life and believed that the practice would lead to abuses, and, being illegal, would be regarded as murder. Many others continued to see life as God's gift, not to be taken lightly or curtailed prematurely.

Thus many people believed that the issue could not be settled in light of moral and religious concerns, and more attention was given to its legal aspects. As a compromise, some people began to advocate what they called "passive euthanasia." At that time, the term referred to the avoidance of extreme or heroic measures to prolong life in cases of incurable and painful illness; advocates maintained that treatment should be withheld not to hasten death but to avoid the pain and suffering of prolonged dying. This development paved the way for more contemporary controversies surrounding the issue of withdrawing medical treatment, which today is associated with the term "passive euthanasia."

The line between active killing for mercy and withdrawing or withholding medical treatment has been, until recently, a critical part of an ethic for the care of the terminally or critically ill. With recent cases in which decisions to withdraw medically supplied nutrition and hydration are legally sanctioned, people are raising questions about the validity of the sharp moral and legal distinction between passive and active euthanasia.

CHAPTER 1

EUTHANASIA IN PRACTICE: THE CASE OF THE NETHERLANDS

READING

2

THE LEGAL STATUS AND PRACTICE OF EUTHANASIA IN HOLLAND

U.S. House Subcommittee on the Constitution

The U.S. House of Representatives Subcommittee on the Constitution of the Judiciary Committee is chaired by Charles T. Canady (R-FL). The report released by the committee examines the legal developments and policy arguments justifying the practice of euthanasia in the Netherlands.

■ POINTS TO CONSIDER

1. Explain the legal status of euthanasia in the Netherlands.

2. How do the Dutch understand "euthanasia," according to the reading? Does this definition differ from yours?

3. Contrast the 1981 Rotterdam case with the 1982 Alkmaar case and discuss the significance of the differences.

4. Discuss the position of the Royal Dutch Physicians Association in the contemporary euthanasia debate.

5. Summarize the latest criteria for performing euthanasia. What do you think of these?

Excerpted from a report of the U.S. House of Representatives Subcommittee of the Constitution of the Judiciary Committee entitled, "Physician-Assisted Suicide in the Netherlands," September 1996.

Euthanasia technically remains illegal under Article 293 of the Dutch Penal Code. However, as in the past, it is rare that a physician would be prosecuted for a violation of Article 293.

Since 1886, Articles 293 and 294 of the Dutch Penal Code have prohibited euthanasia by request and assisted suicide. Article 293 states: "He who robs another of life at his express and serious wish, is punished with a prison sentence of at most twelve years or a fine of the fifth category (a maximum of approximately $50,000)." Article 294 prohibits assisted suicide. The Article states: "He who deliberately incites another to suicide, assists him therein or provides him with the means, is punished, if the suicide follows, with a prison sentence of at most three years or a fine of the fourth category (a maximum of approximately $12,500)."

THE DUTCH PENAL CODE

The Dutch Penal Code recognizes a difference between taking life against an individual's will and taking life at the request of the individual and decreases the punishment for the latter. In the first circumstance, the law punishes both the crime of taking the life from the individual and the crime of taking a life from the community. In the second circumstance, the law punishes only for the crime against the community. Articles 293 and 294 have remained unchanged since 1886. The statutory prohibitions against assisted suicide and euthanasia have never been abolished or amended.

THE BEGINNING OF EUTHANASIA IN THE NETHERLANDS

The public discussion of euthanasia and assisted suicide began in the Netherlands in 1973. The criminal court at Leeuwarden sentenced a physician for administering a fatal injection to her mother. The court established criteria for the administering of drugs which could shorten a patient's life, but required the goal of the treatment to be relief of physical or psychic pain. The court required that the patient be suffering unbearable physical or psychic pain from an incurable, terminal illness. The physician in the case was found guilty because she had directly administered a lethal injection with the goal of terminating the patient's life. Still, the court imposed only a suspended prison sentence of one week.

Also in 1973, the medical profession's primary representative organization, the Royal Dutch Medical Association (KNMG), issued a statement that paralleled the Leeuwarden court decision. The statement concluded that euthanasia should remain prohibited under Article 293, but that combating pain and discontinuing futile treatment could be justified, even if the patient died as the result of the act or omission.

EVOLUTION OF ACCEPTABLE PRACTICE

Eight years later in 1981, the court at Rotterdam convicted a layperson of assisting a terminally ill person in suicide. In the court's decision, nine criteria were listed that, if met, would justify not only assisted suicide, but also the performance of active euthanasia: (1) The patient must be suffering unbearably; (2) the patient must be conscious when he expresses the desire to die; (3) the request for euthanasia must be voluntary; (4) the patient must have been given alternatives with time to consider them; (5) there must be viable solutions for the patient; (6) the death does not inflict unnecessary suffering on others; (7) the decision must involve more than one person; (8) only a physician may perform the euthanasia; and (9) the physician must exercise great care in making the decision. The defendant in the case was convicted because he was not a physician.

In 1982, the court at Alkmaar considered the case of a physician who euthanized a ninety-five-year-old woman who was in deteriorating health. The court found that the patient had a broad right to self-determination and that her request for euthanasia fell within that right. The physician in the case was acquitted, but then was convicted by the Court of Appeals at Amsterdam. The appeals court argued that the physician was subject to Article 293 and had failed to show that he fell under an exception to the code because he could not demonstrate that he was unable to alleviate the patient's suffering in a way other than euthanasia. The physician appealed to the Supreme Court.

The KNMG changed its official stance shortly before the decision of the Supreme Court in the Alkmaar case, and since then, has taken an active role in legitimizing euthanasia in the Netherlands. The association released a report describing criteria which, if met, would justify euthanasia. The criteria in the report were very similar to the criteria subsequently discussed by the Court.

In 1984 the Supreme Court of the Netherlands heard the Alkmaar case. The Court held that "necessity" pursuant to Article

40 of the Penal Code is a defense for a physician accused of euthanasia on request. Article 40 of the Dutch Penal Code provides a defense for a person who commits an offense as a result of "irresistible compulsion or necessity."

DEVELOPING GUIDELINES

In 1985, the State Commission on Euthanasia, which had been formed and charged with recommending legislative reforms on euthanasia, released a report. The majority of the commission believed that there were circumstances under which euthanasia was justifiable. The report suggested that euthanasia be restricted to cases in which the patient, who voluntarily consented, was suffering unbearably and had no other medical alternative. Although some members of the commission wanted euthanasia restricted to those patients who were dying, the report did not include such a recommendation. The report also suggested that there were cases, such as persistent vegetative state, in which the patient did not consent to the euthanasia, but the act would be justified. The actual legislative reform recommended by the commission was amending Article 293 to allow euthanasia for competent, conscious patients who request the act. No such legislation passed, and euthanasia technically remained punishable.

In 1986, the Supreme Court heard its second case on euthanasia. The case involved a physician who administered a lethal dose of morphine to a seventy-three-year-old woman at her request who was chronically ill in the advanced stages of multiple sclerosis. The district court found the accused guilty but because of mitigating circumstances, imposed no punishment. The appellate court affirmed the judgment of the district court but imposed a suspended sentence of two months with two years of probation. The Supreme Court vacated the sentence and referred the case to a lower court for further action consistent with its opinion. While the Court refused to go so far as to set aside Article 293 for physicians, it explicitly held that euthanasia could be justified for a non-terminal patient if the patient was under dire distress or if the physician was acting out of necessity and mental duress.

Also in 1986, the KNMG in collaboration with the National Association of Nurses established "Guidelines for Euthanasia." The Guidelines are based on the 1984 report of the KNMG. The definition of euthanasia in the Guidelines is the generally accepted definition in the Netherlands: "'euthanasia' only covers intentional mercy killing on request, and the act is always an 'active' one." Under this definition, non-voluntary mercy killing is not considered to be euthanasia. The Guidelines also exclude from the definition of euthanasia: withdrawal or withholding medically futile treatment; treatment to alleviate pain and suffering that has the side effect of the patient dying sooner; and the patient refusing to consent to treatment.

There are five criteria that serve as the 1986 Guidelines for justifying euthanasia: "voluntariness," "a well considered request," "persistent desire for death," "unacceptable suffering," and "collegial consultation."

NON-VOLUNTARY EUTHANASIA

In 1989, the Dutch Supreme Court heard the case of a physician who gave a lethal injection to a newborn baby with Down's syndrome. The child was born with an intestinal atresia, a relatively common and repairable problem. The issue for the Court was whether the physician's objection to being prosecuted was justifiable. The Court decided that since the child would have experienced very serious suffering after surgery, it was not likely that the physician would be convicted if his case went to court, and therefore, his objection to prosecution was justified. This case effectively extended the necessity defense to non-voluntary euthanasia.

A study commissioned in January of 1990 confirmed that non-voluntary euthanasia was being performed in the Netherlands. The Dutch Government formed a commission to study the practice of euthanasia, assisted suicide and other end of life decisions in the Netherlands. The Attorney General of the Supreme Court of the Netherlands, Professor Remmelink, appointed and chaired the commission. The commission surveyed physicians about "the practice of action and inaction by a doctor that may lead to the end of a patient's life at this patient's explicit and serious request or otherwise," and published its findings, the "Remmelink Report," in September of 1991.

The commission found that in 1990 there were 2,300 cases of euthanasia (defined as "the deliberate termination of another's life at his request"), 400 cases of assisted suicide, and more than 1,000 cases of life termination without an explicit request. The last number, the euthanizing of 1,000 patients without their request, was somewhat unexpected by the commission. Still the commission justified these "deliberate life-terminating actions without explicit request" by stating, "The ultimate justification for the intervention is in both cases the patient's unbearable suffering. So, medically speaking, there is little difference between these situations and euthanasia, because in both cases patients are involved who suffer terribly."

The commission did not address the fact that the criterion of "unbearable suffering" had in the past been a subjective measurement made by the patient. Nor did the commission address their finding that 14 percent of the patients who were euthanized without consent were fully competent and 11 percent were partially competent.

Based on the findings of the Remmelink Report and the 1986 Guidelines on Euthanasia, the Government established, and both Houses of Parliament approved, a new reporting procedure which was codified and became effective on June 1, 1994. The reporting procedure applies to euthanasia on request, assisted suicide and euthanasia without the request of the patient. When a physician engages in one of these acts, he must fill out a questionnaire and notify the coroner.

The new reporting procedure does not bring about any fundamental change in the legality of euthanasia in the Netherlands. Euthanasia technically remains illegal under Article 293 of the Dutch Penal Code. However, as in the past, it is rare that a physician would be prosecuted for a violation of Article 293.

MENTAL SUFFERING

The most recent Dutch Supreme Court decision on euthanasia was the 1994 case of Dr. Boudewijn Chabot, a psychiatrist. Dr. Chabot assisted one of his patients, who was a fifty-year-old physically healthy woman, in suicide. Dr. Chabot describes his patient, Mrs. B, in this way:

> She was a 50-year-old social worker. She was also a painter in her spare time. She was divorced. She had been physically abused by her former husband for many years. She had two sons. One son, Peter, died by suicide in 1986, at the age of 20. She then underwent psychiatric treatment for a marriage crisis following his suicide. At that time, she strongly wished to commit suicide, but decided that her second son, Robbie, age 15, needed her as a mother.

Her son, Robbie, died of cancer in 1991, at the age of 20. Before his death she decided that she did not want to continue living after he died. She attempted suicide, but did not succeed. On July 13, 1991, she wrote to a social worker at the academic hospital where her second son died of cancer; she asked for a contact and for pills, so that she could kill herself. She had bought a cemetery plot for her sons, her former husband, and herself; her only wish was to die and lie between the two graves of her sons.

Mrs. B objected to both bereavement therapy and anti-depressant drugs; consequently Dr. Chabot administered no treatment but assisted her in suicide. Dr. Chabot contends, "Intolerable psychological suffering is no different from intolerable physical suffering." In his case, the Court reaffirmed that the defense of necessity applies in cases of euthanasia and described the circumstances surrounding an act of necessity:

> The perpetrator of this act, must have had to choose between mutually conflicting obligations and chose the most important one. A physician can in particular be in a state of necessity, when he has to choose between, on the one hand, the obligation to preserve life and, on the other hand, the obligation of a physician to do everything possible to relieve unbearable suffering, for which there is no prospect of improvement whatsoever.

The Court further held that there were physically healthy patients whose unbearable psychological suffering could not be alleviated and extended the defense of necessity to cases in which there is no physical illness. Ultimately, the Court did find Dr. Chabot guilty because he did not arrange for an independent physician to examine Mrs. B in person, but it imposed no punishment.

CONCLUSION

The acceptance in the Netherlands of a right to physician-assisted suicide for terminally ill, competent patients has led the Dutch to embrace physician-assisted suicide for the chronically ill, the elderly and those who are suffering mentally.

Recent legal developments in the United States have driven this country to a crossroads—similar to that faced in the Netherlands in the 1970s and early 1980s—regarding whether physician-assisted suicide will be an accepted practice. The lessons to be learned from the Dutch experience are instructive, and should serve as the vital predicate to an informed discussion about public policy or legislation which may be needed to address this important issue.

22

READING

3

EUTHANASIA IN THE NETHERLANDS: THE POINT

Marcia Angel, M.D.

Marcia Angel, M.D., is the editor of The New England Journal of Medicine. *The following editorial was written after the release of the 1995 Dutch Study comparing euthanasia reporting compliance post-1994 to the findings of the 1990 Remmelink Report. The U.S. Supreme Court was also preparing to hear arguments in early 1997 on assisted suicide laws in New York and Washington State.*

■ POINTS TO CONSIDER

1. How will the results of the Remmelink study be interpreted by the polar sides of the assisted-suicide debate in the U.S., according to Dr. Angel?

2. Summarize the results of the Dutch study commissioned in 1995. How does the author interpret these results?

3. Analyze the statements in the reading related to non-voluntary euthanasia. Does the author believe the Netherlands is more prone to this practice than other countries?

4. Compare and contrast the understanding of euthanasia in the U.S. and the Netherlands. Also, summarize the author's comparison of end-of-life medical practices in the U.S. and the Netherlands. What are the implications of this?

Angel, Marcia, M.D. "Euthanasia in the Netherlands – Good News or Bad?" **The New England Journal of Medicine**, vol. 335, no. 22. November 28, 1996: 1676-8. Copyright © 1996 Massachusetts Medical Society. All rights reserved.

As far as we can tell, Dutch physicians continue to practice physician-assisted dying only reluctantly and under compelling circumstances.

EUTHANASIA GUIDELINES

Euthanasia (the deliberate administration of a lethal drug to hasten death in a suffering patient) is officially a crime in the Netherlands, punishable by up to 12 years in prison, but its practice has been accepted there for over 20 years, protected by a body of case law and strong public support. Adding to the legal ambiguity, the Royal Dutch Medical Association issued guidelines for the practice of euthanasia in 1984, and they were endorsed by a government-appointed commission on euthanasia a year later. The guidelines require that four conditions be met before euthanasia is performed: (1) the patient must be a mentally competent adult; (2) the patient must request euthanasia voluntarily, consistently, and repeatedly over a reasonable time, and the request must be documented; (3) the patient must be suffering intolerably, with no prospect of relief, although the disease need not be terminal; and (4) the doctor must consult with another physician not involved in the case. The usual method of euthanasia is the induction of sleep with a barbiturate, followed by a lethal injection of curare. Doctors who follow the guidelines are rarely prosecuted, but there are no guarantees, and it is generally acknowledged that most doctors who perform euthanasia do not report it, but instead ascribe the death to natural causes. Thus, until 1990, the true frequency of euthanasia in the Netherlands and the circumstances under which it occurred remained unclear. There were, however, many anecdotes about violations of the guidelines, including instances of euthanasia being performed without the patient's request.

THE REMMELINK STUDY

Because so little was known about the practice of euthanasia, the Dutch government in 1990 appointed a commission, headed by Professor Jan Remmelink, the attorney general of the Dutch Supreme Court, to oversee a careful, nationwide study of the practice. In 1991, the investigators reported their findings. Of the roughly 130,000 deaths in the Netherlands in 1990, they estimated from physician interviews and questionnaires that 2300 (1.8 percent) were the result of euthanasia. Another 400 deaths (0.3

24

percent) were assisted suicides. Only 486 physician-assisted deaths (euthanasia or assisted suicide) had been reported as such on the death certificate. In nearly all of these 2700 cases, the guidelines seemed to be met, despite the fact that the cases were usually not reported. However, in an additional 1000 deaths (0.8 percent), the patient was not competent when euthanasia was performed – a clear violation of the guidelines (the Dutch do not even use the term "euthanasia" for this practice, reserving it for strictly voluntary cases).

Those looking to the Netherlands as a bellwether in the growing debate about physician-assisted dying in the United States seized on the Remmelink report, but both sides claimed that the results supported their position. To those opposed to assisted suicide or euthanasia, the fact that 1000 of 3300 cases of euthanasia in the Netherlands involved incompetent patients meant that allowing any easing of restrictions on physician-assisted dying would surely lead to abuses. We would, like the Dutch, be on a moral slippery slope, with no hope of stopping a rapid slide to the bottom. What would the bottom be? Opponents of physician-assisted dying painted a picture of widespread involuntary euthanasia performed on the very old, the very young, the disabled, and those who were financially costly or otherwise burdensome.

REASSURING RESULTS

To those who favored some form of physician-assisted dying in the United States, however, the results of the Remmelink report were reassuring. First, euthanasia accounted for only a small fraction of total deaths in the Netherlands. Furthermore, it was found to be performed in fewer than a third of those who requested it, indicating that doctors generally were reluctant to accede to such requests. And as far as could be determined in this careful study, euthanasia was performed almost entirely on those who were terminally ill; 87 percent of the patients were expected to die within a week, and another 12 percent in a month.

But what about the 1000 patients who were not competent at the time euthanasia was performed? Wasn't this evidence of abuse or worse? According to the Remmelink study, over half had earlier expressed an interest in euthanasia, while competent, and most were moribund at the time euthanasia was performed. This information, however, was drawn from interviews with doctors, not necessarily an accurate source in such cases, for obvious reasons.

The fact that doctors, granted confidentiality, were so willing to acknowledge that they had performed euthanasia without reporting it offers some internal evidence of candor. Still, it is possible that there were also cases of involuntary euthanasia under less compelling circumstances, and that doctors did not reveal them to the interviewers. But such cases could occur in any country, and there is no reason to believe they are more common in the Netherlands than elsewhere.

COMPLIANCE TO GUIDELINES

A second nationwide investigation of physician-assisted dying in the Netherlands was commissioned in 1995. It consisted of two major studies. The first compared the practices in 1995 with those in 1990 to see whether the country was indeed sliding down a slippery slope with regard to medical care at the end of life. The second sought to evaluate the adequacy of a new notification procedure. This procedure for reporting and reviewing cases of physician-assisted death was formulated by the Ministry of Justice and the Royal Dutch Medical Association at the time the Remmelink Commission was formed, and became law in 1994. It was intended to enable better monitoring of euthanasia and physician-assisted suicide and to ensure public accountability.

INCREASED NOTIFICATION

Are the Dutch on a slippery slope? It appears not. The first report, by van der Maas and colleagues, shows that the practices in 1995 were not much different from those in 1990. Euthanasia was somewhat more frequent, but the authors believe that this can be partly explained by the aging of the population and the increased mortality from cancer, the usual underlying disease in cases of euthanasia. Assisted suicide remained rare, perhaps because it is slower than euthanasia and because the Dutch draw no moral distinction between the two acts. As in 1990, nearly all cases of euthanasia involved patients who were suffering from terminal illness and had only a short time to live. The incidence of ending life without an explicit request from the patient – the most disturbing finding in the earlier study – was slightly less in 1995 than in 1990. It would be very hard to construe these findings as a descent into depravity. As far as we can tell, Dutch physicians continue to practice physician-assisted dying only reluctantly and under compelling circumstances.

As for the notification procedure, the results were mixed.

26

Life-support system?

Cartoon by David Seavey. Copyright, **USA TODAY.**
Reprinted with permission.

Van der Maas and colleagues show that the fraction of physician-assisted deaths that were reported increased greatly, from 18 percent in 1990 to 41 percent in 1995. Still, the majority of cases continued to go unreported. Although most doctors said they thought some sort of oversight of cases of physician-assisted death was appropriate, they found the new procedure, with its multiple levels of legal review, burdensome. Furthermore, many doctors found it troublesome that euthanasia remains a crime, despite the official status of the guidelines and the legal reporting requirements. Although the risk of prosecution is exceedingly small, doctors who perform euthanasia may not wish to take any chances or to undergo scrutiny under such legally ambiguous conditions. It is likely that the rate of reporting will remain low unless the notification procedure is made less daunting and the peculiar legal situation is clarified. Ultimately, it is untenable for a medical practice to be simultaneously legal and illegal.

NO MEANINGFUL COMPARISONS

How does the Dutch experience compare with practice in the United States? It is virtually impossible to draw any meaningful comparisons. In the United States, euthanasia is illegal in all states, and assisting suicide is illegal in most; unlike a Dutch doctor, an American doctor could expect vigorous prosecution for euthanasia and the possibility of it for assisting suicide, the failure to convict Dr. Jack Kevorkian notwithstanding. Thus, our only way of gaining information on these practices is through surveys that promise anonymity – a notoriously inaccurate way to gain information about the frequency of a crime for which prosecution is likely. Nevertheless, in a recent survey of physicians in the state of Washington, 12 percent said they had in the past year been asked to assist in a patient's suicide and four percent said they had been asked to perform euthanasia; they claim to have granted a quarter of the requests – interestingly, about the same fraction as granted in the Netherlands.

Care at the end of life involves some of the most wrenching decisions in medicine. In this country, we have a solid medical and legal consensus that permits forgoing life-prolonging treatment at the request of a patient or surrogate. According to an estimate by the American Hospital Association, about 70 percent of hospital deaths in the United States occur after a decision has been made to forgo treatment. We also permit the use of opioids to treat pain or breathlessness in doses that might predictably shorten life, although we have no data as to how often this practice contributes to death. Van der Maas and colleagues report that forgoing life-prolonging treatment preceded about 20 percent of all deaths in the Netherlands in 1995, fewer than in the United States, and the use of possibly life-shortening doses of opioids to treat symptoms preceded about 17.5 percent of deaths. In both countries, then, these practices are not only legal, but also common. But until recently, physician-assisted dying has been considered in the United States to be quite different, a violation of medical ethics as well as the law. Yet there will remain patients who are suffering unbearably from irreversible disease, whose symptoms are intractable, and for whom there is no life-sustaining treatment to forgo. What about them? Do they have no right to ask their doctors for help in ending their lives peacefully?

GERMAN INSIGHTS

That the Germans view aid-in-dying issues differently from the Dutch is little surprise, given their quite opposite histories in the Second World War. In the minds of most Germans, the very term *euthanasia* is associated with the Nazis, and, in general, it is understood as involuntary killing on potentially political rather than medical grounds. Rejection of euthanasia may also be associated with distrust of physicians in an authoritarian medical climate....

The situation with respect to assisted suicide in Germany is marked by two important features. For one thing, the practice is both legal and partly institutionalized; it occurs on a much larger scale and in different ways than in Holland, and of course occurs in a way not currently possible in the United States. Second, the practice of assisted suicide in Germany is embedded in a distinctive cultural climate...Not only do patients with terminal illnesses have different options concerning suicide in Germany than they do in the U.S.; they also are able to talk differently about it as well....

Freitod (literally "free death" or "voluntary death") is a positive term, free from connotations of either moral wrongness or pathology...

Margaret P. Battin, "Assisted Suicide: Can We Learn from Germany?" **The Hastings Center Report**. March 1992.

GROWING SUPPORT

That is the question that will be argued before the U.S. Supreme Court in January 1997. Unlike the situation in the Netherlands, the focus will be on physician-assisted suicide, not on euthanasia. Support for decriminalizing assisted suicide has been growing, whereas support for euthanasia remains weak. This reflects the fact that we tend to draw a moral distinction between euthanasia and assisting suicide that the Dutch do not. Of greater practical consequence is the fact that euthanasia can be involuntary, whereas suicide, by definition, must be voluntary. That is important in the United States, where, because of our greater disparities in socioeconomic status and the high cost of medical care, the risk of abuse of euthanasia is undoubtedly greater than it is in the Netherlands. Assisted suicide is considered less liable to abuse. For these reasons, if any form of physician-assisted dying becomes accepted in the United States, it is likely to be assisted suicide, not euthanasia.

Recently, the Ninth Circuit Court of Appeals (with jurisdiction over California, Alaska, Arizona, Hawaii, Idaho, Montana, Nevada, Oregon, and Washington) and the Second Circuit Court of Appeals (with jurisdiction over New York, Connecticut, and Vermont) each struck down state laws forbidding physician-assisted suicide. Although the rationale was somewhat different in the two decisions, both argued that the state laws violated constitutionally guaranteed rights. These are the cases the Supreme Court has agreed to review. Whatever the decision, it will no doubt be as contentious as any since *Roe v. Wade.* The two studies from the Netherlands offer some insight into the practice of physician-assisted dying in a country that openly permits it. As with the 1990 study from the Netherlands, however, both sides in the American debate will most likely claim that the findings support their position as the controversy intensifies and the matter comes before our highest court.

LESSONS FROM THE DUTCH FAILURE: THE COUNTERPOINT

Herbert Hendin, M.D.

Herbert Hendin, M.D., is a professor of psychiatry at New York Medical College and the executive director of the American Suicide Foundation, New York.

■ POINTS TO CONSIDER

1. How does the author interpret the data from the Remmelink Study?

2. Explain the "slippery slope" argument.

3. Discuss Dr. Hendin's point concerning external pressure on patients considering euthanasia.

4. Describe the consequences of legal rights to euthanasia or physician-assisted suicide, according to the reading.

Excerpted from the testimony of Herbert Hendin, M.D., before the Subcommittee of the Constitution of the U.S. House of Representatives Judiciary Committee, April 29, 1996.

Once the Dutch accepted assisted suicide, it was not possible legally or morally to deny more active medical help, i.e., euthanasia, to those who could not effect their own deaths.

In the past decade by making assisted suicide and euthanasia easily available, the Dutch have significantly reduced the suicide rate of those over fifty in the population. The likelihood that patients would end their own lives if euthanasia was not available to them was one of the justifications given by Dutch doctors for providing such help.

CURE FOR SUICIDE?

Of course, euthanasia advocates can maintain that making suicide "unnecessary" for those over fifty who are physically ill is a benefit of legalization rather than a sign of abuse. Such an attitude depends, of course, on whether one believes that there are alternatives to assisted suicide or euthanasia for dealing with the problems of older people who become ill.

Among an older population, physical illness of all types is common, and many who have trouble coping with physical illness became suicidal. In a culture accepting of euthanasia their distress may be accepted as a legitimate reason for euthanasia. It may be more than ironic to describe euthanasia as "the Dutch cure for suicide."

That seems even more true since the Dutch have recently accepted mental suffering without physical illness as justification for assisted suicide and euthanasia. How this acceptance translates into practice with a psychiatric patient is evident in a case that has received a good deal of international attention since it was the case that formally established in the Netherlands that mental suffering was sufficient justification for assisted suicide.

PSYCHIATRIC ILLNESS

In the spring of 1993 a Dutch court in Assen ruled that a psychiatrist was justified in assisting in the suicide of his patient, a physically healthy but grief-stricken 50-year-old social worker who was mourning the death of her son and who came to the psychiatrist saying she wanted death, not treatment. I had a chance to spend about seven hours interviewing the psychiatrist involved. Without going into the details of the case, it is worth noting that the psychiatrist assisted in the patient's suicide a little over two months after she came to see him, about four months after her younger son died of cancer at age 20. Discussion of the case centered around whether the psychiatrist, supported by experts, was right in his contention that the woman suffered from an understandable and untreatable grief. Although no one should underestimate the grief of a mother who has lost a beloved child, life offers ways to cope with such grief, and time alone was likely to have altered her mood.

The Dutch Supreme Court which ruled on the Assen Case in June 1994 agreed with the lower courts in affirming that mental suffering can be grounds for euthanasia, but felt that in the absence of physical illness a psychiatric consultant should have actually seen the patient. Since it felt that in all other regards the psychiatrist had behaved responsibly, it imposed no punishment. Since the consultation can easily be obtained from a sympathetic colleague, it offers the patient little protection. The case was seen as a triumph by euthanasia advocates since it legally established mental suffering as a basis for euthanasia.

SLIPPERY SLOPE

Over the past two decades, the Netherlands has moved from assisted suicide to euthanasia, from euthanasia for the terminally ill to euthanasia for the chronically ill, from euthanasia for physical illness to euthanasia for psychological distress and from voluntary euthanasia to non-voluntary and involuntary euthanasia.

Once the Dutch accepted assisted suicide, it was not possible legally or morally to deny more active medical help, i.e., euthanasia, to those who could not effect their own deaths. Nor could they deny assisted suicide or euthanasia to the chronically ill who have longer to suffer than the terminally ill or to those who have psychological pain not associated with physical disease. To do so would be a form of discrimination. Involuntary euthanasia has been justified as necessitated by the need to make decisions for patients not competent to choose for themselves.

That it is often the doctor and not the patient who determines the choice for death was underlined by the documentation of "involuntary euthanasia" in the Remmelink report — the Dutch government's commissioned study of the problem. "Involuntary euthanasia" is a term that is disturbing to the Dutch. The Dutch define euthanasia as the ending of the life of one person by another at the first person's request. If life is ended without request they do not consider it to be euthanasia. The Remmelink report uses the equally troubling expression "termination of the patient's life without explicit request" to refer to euthanasia performed without consent on competent, partially competent, and incompetent patients.

REMMELINK REPORT

The report revealed that in over 1,000 cases, of the 130,000 deaths in the Netherlands each year, physicians admitted they actively caused or hastened death without any request from the patient. In about 25,000 cases, medical decisions were made at the end of life that might have been or were intended to end the life of the patient without consulting the patient. In nearly 20,000 of these cases (about 80 percent) physicians gave the patient's impaired ability to communicate as their justification for not seeking consent.

This left about 5,000 cases in which physicians made decisions that might have been or were intended to end the lives of competent patients without consulting them. In 13 percent of these cases, physicians who did not communicate with competent patients concerning decisions that might have been or were intended to end their lives gave as a reason for not doing so that they had previously had some discussion of the subject with the patient. Yet it seems incomprehensible that a physician would terminate the life of a competent patient on the basis of some prior discussion without checking if the patient still felt the same way.

BYPASSING ADEQUATE CONSULTATION

A number of Dutch euthanasia advocates have admitted that practicing euthanasia with legal sanction has encouraged doctors to feel that they can make life or death decisions without consulting patients. Many advocates privately defend the need for doctors to end the lives of competent patients without discussion with them. An attorney who represents the Dutch Voluntary Euthanasia Society gave me as an example a case in which a doctor had terminated the life of a nun a few days before she would have died because she was in excruciating pain but her religious convictions did not permit her to ask for death. He did not argue when I asked why she should not have been permitted to die in the way she wanted.

Even when the patient requests or consents to euthanasia, in cases presented to me in the Netherlands and cases I have reviewed in this country, assisted suicide and euthanasia were usually the result of an interaction in which the needs and character of family, friends, and doctor play as big and often bigger role than those of the patient.

OUTSIDE PRESSURE

In a study of euthanasia done in Dutch hospitals, doctors and nurses reported that more requests for euthanasia came from families than from patients themselves. The investigator concluded that the families, the doctors, and the nurses were involved in pressuring patients to request euthanasia.

A Dutch medical journal noted an example of a wife who no longer wished to care for her sick husband; she gave him a choice between euthanasia and admission to a home for the chronically ill. The man, afraid of being left to the mercy of strangers in an unfamiliar place, chose to be killed. The doctor, although aware of the coercion, ended the man's life.

The Remmelink report revealed that more than half of Dutch physicians considered it appropriate to introduce the subject of euthanasia to their patients. Virtually all the medical advocates of euthanasia that I spoke to in the Netherlands saw this as enabling the patient to consider an option that he or she may have felt inhibited about bringing up, rather than a form of coercion. They seemed not to recognize that the doctor was also telling the patient that his or her life was not worth living, a message that would have a powerful effect on the patient's outlook and decision.

PALLIATIVE CARE WILL SUFFER

The Dutch experience illustrates how social sanction promotes a culture that transforms suicide into assisted suicide and euthanasia and encourages patients and doctors to see assisted suicide and euthanasia — intended as an unfortunate necessity in exceptional cases — as almost a routine way of dealing with serious or terminal illness.

Pressure for improved palliative care appears to have evaporated in the Netherlands. Discussion of care for the terminally ill is dominated by how and when to extend assisted suicide and euthanasia to increasing groups of patients. Given the inequities in our own health care system and the inadequacies of our care of those who are terminally ill, palliative care would be an even more likely casualty of euthanasia in this country. Euthanasia will become a way for all of us to ignore the genuine needs of terminally ill people.

The public has the illusion that legalizing assisted suicide and euthanasia will give them greater autonomy. If the Dutch experience teaches us anything, it is that the reverse is true. In practice it is still the doctor who decides whether to perform euthanasia. He can suggest it, not give patients obvious alternatives, ignore patients' ambivalence, and even put to death patients who have not requested it. Euthanasia enhances the power and control of doctors, not patients.

People assume that the doctor encouraging or supporting assisted suicide is making as objective a judgment as a radiologist reading an x-ray. The decisive role of the physician's needs and values in the decision for euthanasia are not apparent to them.

VIOLATION, ABUSE

Virtually every guideline set up by the Dutch to regulate euthanasia has been modified or violated with impunity. Despite their best efforts, the Dutch have been able to get only 60 percent of their doctors to report their euthanasia cases (and there is reason from the Remmelink report to question whether all of them are reporting truthfully). Since following the legal guidelines would free from the risk of prosecution the 40 percent of Dutch doctors who admit to not reporting their cases and the 20 percent who say that under no circumstances will they do so, it is a reasonable assumption that these doctors are not following the guidelines.

A supervisory system intended to protect patients would require an ombudsman to look at the overall situation including the family, the patient, the doctor, and, above all, the interaction among them prior to the performance of assisted suicide or euthanasia. This would involve an intrusion into the relationship between patient and doctor that most patients would not want and most doctors would not accept.

NAZI RESISTANCE

There is a bitter irony to what is happening in Holland. During the World War II German occupation of the Netherlands, fully 98% of that country's physicians refused to join a German-sponsored medical organization that was headed by a Nazi sympathizer and an anti-Semite. The Dutch doctors took down their shingles and refused to practice although they were aware that such actions could subject them to severe punishments.

Excerpted from the testimony of Rabbi A. James Rudin before the Subcommittee on Health and Environment of the U.S. House of Representatives Committee on Commerce, March 6, 1997.

LESSONS FROM THE DUTCH FAILURE

Without such intrusion before the fact, there is no law or set of guidelines that can protect patients. After euthanasia has been performed, since only the patient and the doctor may know the actual facts of the case, and since only the doctor is alive to relate them, any medical, legal, or interdisciplinary review committee will, as in the Netherlands, only know what the doctor chooses to tell them. Legal sanction creates a permissive atmosphere that seems to foster not taking the guidelines too seriously. The notion that those American doctors – who are admittedly breaking some serious laws in now assisting in a suicide – would follow guidelines if assisted suicide were legalized is not borne out by the Dutch experience; nor is it likely given the failure of American practitioners of assisted suicide to follow elementary safeguards in cases they have published.

INTERPRETING EDITORIAL CARTOONS

This activity may be used as an individualized study guide for students in libraries and resource centers or as a discussion catalyst in small group and classroom discussions.

Although cartoons are usually humorous, the main intent of most political cartoonists is not to entertain. Cartoons express serious social comment about important issues. Using graphic and visual arts, the cartoonist expresses opinions and attitudes. By employing an entertaining and often light-hearted visual format, cartoonists may have as much or more impact on national and world issues as editorial and syndicated columnists.

■ POINTS TO CONSIDER

1. Examine the cartoon in this chapter.

2. How would you describe the message of the cartoon? Try to describe the message in one to three sentences.

3. Do you agree with the message expressed in the cartoon? Why or why not?

4. Are any of the readings in Chapter One in basic agreement with the cartoon?

CHAPTER 2

THE OREGON LAW

READING

5

THE OREGON LAW

Oregon Right to Die

Ballot Measure 16, The Oregon Death with Dignity Act, passed in a state referendum November 8, 1994. Authored by Oregon Right to Die, the act allows physicians to prescribe lethal doses of drugs to competent, terminally ill adults. Since the popular vote, the law has been challenged in Federal Court and turned back to Oregon voters for repeal (see chronology). The following is an excerpt from the Oregon Death with Dignity Act, sections two and three. Oregon Right to Die is a political action committee, concentrating on end-of-life issues. Since its founding in 1993, the primary focus of the organization has been the adoption and defense of the Oregon Death with Dignity Act.

■ **POINTS TO CONSIDER**

1. Describe the Oregon Law.

2. What safeguards exist according to the language of the bill?

3. Analyze the law and discuss what opponents may challenge concerning the text of the Death with Dignity Act.

Excerpted from Oregon Rev. Stat. §§ 127.800-127.995, Death with Dignity Act, and excerpted from "Chronology of Oregon Death with Dignity Act," ed. Oregon Right to Die, July, 1998. Reprinted by permission, Oregon Right to Die, 625 SW 10th Ave., Ste. 349C, Portland, OR 97205.

An adult who is capable may make a written request for medication for the purpose of ending his or her life in a humane and dignified manner in accordance with this Act.

SECTION 2

WRITTEN REQUEST FOR MEDICATION TO END ONE'S LIFE IN A HUMANE AND DIGNIFIED MANNER

§ 2.01 Who May Initiate a Written Request for Medication

An adult who is capable, is a resident of Oregon and has been determined by the attending physician and consulting physician to be suffering from a terminal disease, and who has voluntarily expressed his or her wish to die, may make a written request for medication for the purpose of ending his or her life in a humane and dignified manner in accordance with this Act.

§ 2.02 Form of the Written Request

(1) A valid request for medication under this Act shall be in substantially the form described in Section 6 of this Act, signed and dated by the patient and witnessed by at least two individuals who, in the presence of the patient, attest that to the best of their knowledge and belief the patient is capable, acting voluntarily, and is not being coerced to sign the request.

(2) One of the witnesses shall be a person who is not:

(a) A relative of the patient by blood, marriage or adoption;

(b) A person who at the time the request is signed would be entitled to any portion of the estate of the qualified patient upon death under any will or by operation of law; or

(c) An owner, operator or employee of a health care facility where the qualified patient is receiving medical treatment or is a resident.

(3) The patient's attending physician at the time the request is signed shall not be a witness.

(4) If the patient is a patient in a long term care facility at the time the written request is made, one of the witnesses shall be an individual designated by the facility and having the qualifications specified by the Department of Human Resources by rule.

41

SECTION 3

SAFEGUARDS

§ 3.01 Attending Physician Responsibilities

The attending physician shall:

(1) Make the initial determination of whether a patient has a terminal disease, is capable, and has made the request voluntarily;

(2) Inform the patient of:

(a) his or her medical diagnosis;

(b) his or her prognosis;

(c) the potential risks associated with taking the medication to be prescribed;

(d) the probable result of taking the medication to be prescribed;

(e) the feasible alternatives, including, but not limited to, comfort care, hospice care and pain control.

(3) Refer the patient to a consulting physician for medical confirmation of the diagnosis, and for a determination that the patient is capable and acting voluntarily;

(4) Refer the patient for counseling if appropriate pursuant to Section 3.03;

(5) Request that the patient notify next of kin;

(6) Inform the patient that he or she has an opportunity to rescind the request at any time and in any manner, and offer the patient an opportunity to rescind at the end of the 15 day waiting period pursuant to Section 3.06;

(7) Verify, immediately prior to writing the prescription for medication under this Act, that the patient is making an informed decision;

(8) Fulfill the medical record documentation requirements of Section 3.09;

(9) Ensure that all appropriate steps are carried out in accordance with this Act prior to writing a prescription for medication to enable a qualified patient to end his or her life in a humane and

dignified manner.

§ 3.02 Consulting Physician Confirmation

Before a patient is qualified under this Act, a consulting physician shall examine the patient and his or her relevant medical records and confirm, in writing, the attending physician's diagnosis that the patient is suffering from a terminal disease, and verify that the patient is capable, is acting voluntarily and has made an informed decision.

§ 3.03 Counseling Referral

If in the opinion of the attending physician or the consulting physician a patient may be suffering from a psychiatric or psychological disorder, or depression causing impaired judgment, either physician shall refer the patient for counseling. No medication to end a patient's life in a humane and dignified manner shall be prescribed until the person performing the counseling determines that the patient is not suffering from a psychiatric or psychological disorder, or depression causing impaired judgment.

§ 3.04 Informed Decision

No person shall receive a prescription for medication to end his or her life in a humane and dignified manner unless he or she has made an informed decision. Immediately prior to writing a prescription for medication under this Act, the attending physician shall verify that the patient is making an informed decision.

§ 3.05 Family Notification

The attending physician shall ask the patient to notify next of kin of his or her request for medication pursuant to this Act. A patient who declines or is unable to notify next of kin shall not have his or her request denied for that reason.

§ 3.06 Written and Oral Requests

In order to receive a prescription for medication to end his or her life in a humane and dignified manner, a qualified patient shall have made an oral request and a written request, and reiterate the oral request to his or her attending physician no less than fifteen (15) days after making the initial oral request. At the time the qualified patient makes his or her second oral request, the attending physician shall offer the patient an opportunity to rescind the request.

§ 3.07 Right to Rescind Request

A patient may rescind his or her request at any time and in any manner without regard to his or her mental state. No prescription for medication under this Act may be written without the attending physician offering the qualified patient an opportunity to rescind the request.

§ 3.08 Waiting Periods

No less than fifteen (15) days shall elapse between the patient's initial oral request and the writing of a prescription under this Act. No less than 48 hours shall elapse between the patient's written request and the writing of a prescription under this Act.

§ 3.09 Medical Record Documentation Requirements

The following shall be documented or filed in the patient's medical record:

(1) All oral requests by a patient for medication to end his or her life in a humane and dignified manner;

(2) All written requests by a patient for medication to end his or her life in a humane and dignified manner;

(3) The attending physician's diagnosis and prognosis, determination that the patient is capable, acting voluntarily and has made an informed decision;

(4) The consulting physician's diagnosis and prognosis, and verification that the patient is capable, acting voluntarily and has made an informed decision;

(5) A report of the outcome and determinations made during counseling, if performed;

(6) The attending physician's offer to the patient to rescind his or her request at the time of the patient's second oral request pursuant to Section 3.06; and

(7) A note by the attending physician indicating that all requirements under this Act have been met and indicating the steps taken to carry out the request, including a notation of the medication prescribed.

§ 3.10 Residency Requirement

Only requests made by Oregon residents, under this Act, shall be granted.

§ 3.11 Reporting Requirements

(1) The Health Division shall annually review a sample of records maintained pursuant to this Act.

(2) The Health Division shall make rules to facilitate the collection of information regarding compliance with this Act. The information collected shall not be a public record and may not be made available for inspection by the public.

(3) The Health Division shall generate and make available to the public an annual statistical report of information collected under Section 3.11(2) of this Act.

§ 3.12 Effect on Construction of Wills, Contracts and Statutes

(1) No provision in a contract, will or other agreement, whether written or oral, to the extent the provision would affect whether a person may make or rescind a request for medication to end his or her life in a humane and dignified manner, shall be valid.

(2) No obligation owing under any currently existing contract shall be conditioned or affected by the making or rescinding of a request, by a person, for medication to end his or her life in a humane and dignified manner.

§ 3.13 Insurance or Annuity Policies

The sale, procurement, or issuance of any life, health, or accident insurance or annuity policy or the rate charged for any policy shall not be conditioned upon or affected by the making or rescinding of a request, by a person, for medication to end his or her life in a humane and dignified manner. Neither shall a qualified patient's act of ingesting medication to end his or her life in a humane and dignified manner have an effect upon a life, health, or accident insurance or annuity policy.

§ 3.14 Construction of Act

Nothing in this Act shall be construed to authorize a physician or any other person to end a patient's life by lethal injection, mercy killing or active euthanasia. Actions taken in accordance with this Act shall not, for any purpose, constitute suicide, assisted suicide, mercy killing or homicide, under the law.

A CHRONOLOGY OF THE
OREGON DEATH WITH DIGNITY ACT

1993

June 18   Oregon Right to Die forms.

1994

Nov. 8   The voters of the State of Oregon pass Measure 16 (Oregon's Death with Dignity Act) 51%-49%.

Nov. 23   National Right to Life, Inc. files motion for injunction against Measure 16 in Federal District Court.

Dec.   Oregon Death with Dignity Legal Defense and Education Center forms.

Dec. 7   Judge Hogan places a temporary restraining order on Measure 16.

Dec. 12   Oregon Right to Die files a motion on behalf of Measure 16.

Dec. 19   Judge Hogan extends the temporary restraining order at the First Hearing in Eugene, Oregon.

Dec. 27   At the Second Hearing in Eugene, Judge Hogan places a preliminary injunction on Measure 16 until a later hearing.

1995

Jan. 13   Oregon Right to Die files an emergency appeal with the Ninth Circuit Court of Appeals on behalf of a terminally ill person.

Jan. 17   Ninth Circuit denies the emergency appeal, waits for Judge Hogan's ruling.

Feb. 19   At the Third Hearing, Judge Hogan says he can't rule while the Ninth Circuit has an appeal and postpones until March.

Mar. 14   Ninth Circuit Court of Appeals denies the motion for modification of the injunction.

Apr. 18   Judge Hogan listens to oral arguments at the Fourth Hearing, and says he will give his decision in writing.

Aug. 1   Michael Vernon requests that Judge Hogan grant him relief from the injunction. He has met all of the qualifications of Measure 16.

Aug. 3   Judge Hogan rules that Measure 16 is unconstitutional and denies Michael Vernon's appeal.

Nov. 24   Oregon Death with Dignity files its brief with the Ninth Circuit Court of Appeals.

1996

March 6   Ninth Circuit Court of Appeals rules *en banc* in

Compassion in Dying v. The State of Washington that there is a constitutionally protected right for terminally ill persons to determine the manner and timing of their own death as a "liberty interest" under the 14th Amendment to the U.S. Constitution.

March 7   Oregon Death with Dignity files an emergency motion with the Ninth Circuit Court of Appeals asking that the injunction on the Oregon Death with Dignity Act be stayed (lifted).

March 11   The Ninth Circuit Court of Appeals denies Death With Dignity's emergency motion and sends the question back to the district court and Judge Hogan.

April 2   The Second Circuit Court of Appeals rules in Quill v. The State of New York that the right of a terminally ill person to receive a prescription for life-ending medication from a physician is protected under the "equal protection clause" of the 14th Amendment to the U.S. Constitution.

May 9   Judge Hogan denies motion to lift the injunction on the Oregon Death with Dignity Act.

May 17   Oregon Death with Dignity renews its motion to stay the injunction on the Oregon Death with Dignity Act to the Ninth Circuit Court of Appeals.

July 9   The Ninth Circuit Court of Appeals hears oral arguments on the appeal of Judge Hogan's ruling that Measure 16 is unconstitutional.

1997

Jan. 8   The U.S. Supreme Court hears oral arguments on the Washington and New York appeals from both the Ninth and Second Circuit Courts on their decisions of the previous year.

Jan. 28-29 The Family Law Subcommittee of the House Judiciary Committee of the Oregon Legislature holds informational hearings on the possible implementation of the Oregon Death with Dignity Act.

Feb. 17   Seven bills are introduced in the Oregon Legislature to repeal, delay, or alter the Oregon Death with Dignity Act.

Feb. 27   Ninth Circuit Court of Appeals dismisses the lawsuit against Measure 16 and orders Judge Hogan to lift the injunction in 21 days.

Mar. 11-20 The Family Law Subcommittee of the Oregon House Judiciary Committee hears testimony on four of the seven proposed bills dealing with the Oregon Death with Dignity Act.

Mar. 13	The attorney for the National Right to Life, Inc., files a motion with the Ninth Circuit Court of Appeals requesting an *en banc* rehearing of the ruling to lift the injunction on the Act.
April 23	The Family Law Subcommittee of the Oregon House Judiciary Committee votes 4-3 to pass HB 2954, referring Measure 16 back to the voters for repeal at a Nov. 4, 1997, election.
May 2	Full Judiciary Committee of the Oregon House votes 6-4 to pass HB 2954 out to the full House for a vote.
May 13	The Oregon House votes 32-26 to pass HB 2954.
May 27-30	A Special Senate Committee, appointed by the President of the Senate, holds hearings on HB 2954. The Special Committee makes no changes in HB 2954 and passes it out 3-2.
June 9	The Oregon Senate votes 20-10 to pass HB 2954. Because the bill is a referral to the voters, no signature by the Governor is needed and no veto is possible.
June 26	The Supreme Court rules on the Washington and New York cases, that there is no constitutionally protected right to die. The ruling is unanimous. The ruling leaves [the possibility] for further litigation on the issue and says that states may make laws regarding physician-assisted dying.
Oct. 14	The Supreme Court denies *certiori* (refuses to review) the decision of the Ninth Circuit Court of Appeals and thus releases the order that the injunction be lifted from the Oregon Death with Dignity Act.
Oct. 27	The Ninth Circuit Court of Appeals vacates Judge Hogan's injunction. The Oregon Death with Dignity Act goes into effect.
Nov. 4	Oregon voters defeat the attempted repeal of the Act by a 60%-40% margin in the third most expensive initiative campaign in Oregon history.
Nov. 5	Drug Enforcement Administration (DEA) administrator Thomas Constantine, writes a letter to Senator Orrin Hatch (R-Utah) and Republican Henry Hyde (R-IL), stating that if doctors participate under the Oregon Death with Dignity Act, they will be violating the federal Controlled Substances Act (CSA), which could result in the revocation of their licenses. The Attorney General, Janet Reno, says her department has not made an official ruling and will do so after a thorough review.
Nov. 25	Judge Hogan formally dismisses the lawsuit against Measure 16 brought three years before by National Right to

Life, Inc., but allows plaintiffs to brief one more argument.

Nov. 27   Ray Frank is the first person known to have made use of the law. He suffered from kidney and lung cancer. He does not survive the 15-day waiting period.

1998

Jan. 21   An internal Justice Department review team concludes that the federal law does not prohibit doctors from carrying out Oregon's Death with Dignity law. They submit their proposal to the Attorney General.

Feb. 17   In an 11th-hour move, U.S. District Judge Michael Hogan delayed a decision on a challenge to the law. The Right to Life attorney James Bopp finds a second terminally ill patient to join the suit with plaintiff Janice Elsner.

Feb. 26   The Oregon Health Services Commission votes (10-1) to add Oregon's Death with Dignity law to the list of comfort care items covered under the Oregon Health Plan.

Mar. 24   A Portland, Oregon, woman becomes the first known person to use Oregon's Death with Dignity Law. The woman battled breast cancer for 22 years.

June 5   Attorney General Janet Reno releases a Justice Department ruling that says the DEA does not have the authority to revoke the prescribing licenses of Oregon physicians who prescribe life ending medications for terminally ill Oregonians under the guidelines of the Act.

June 5   Representative Henry Hyde (R-IL), House Judiciary Committee Chairman, introduces in the U.S. House of Representatives the "Lethal Drug Abuse Prevention Act of 1998," HB 4006, which amends the Controlled Substances Act to give the DEA the authority that Attorney General Reno had decided it did not have.

July 13   Judge Hogan hears oral arguments from opponents of Death with Dignity trying to revive the lawsuit that was dismissed last year by a federal court of appeals. Hogan will give his decision in writing.

July 15   The House Judiciary Committee's Subcommittee on the Constitution holds hearings on HB 4006. Testifying in opposition to the bill are Oregon Governor John Kitzhaber, M.D., the American Medical Association, the American Pharmaceutical Association, and Oregon's Democratic House members.

July 22   The House Judiciary Committee's Subcommittee on the Constitution passes HB 4006 on to the full Judiciary Committee by a 6-5 vote.

DECRIMINALIZATION IS THE ANSWER

Barbara Coombs Lee

Barbara Coombs Lee was the Chief Petitioner for Oregon's Death with Dignity Act which passed in a November 1994 state referendum.

■ **POINTS TO CONSIDER**

1. Why was the Death with Dignity movement founded? What need does the author cite for physician-assisted suicide?

2. Analyze the base of support for Oregon's Death with Dignity Act, according to the author. Discuss why, in your best estimation, these people or groups would support such an initiative.

3. Summarize the covert activity in which doctors participate, according to the journals cited in the reading.

4. Explain Coombs Lee's belief that decriminalization of assisted suicide is preferable to covert assistance.

Excerpted from the testimony of Barbara Coombs Lee before the Subcommittee on the Constitution of the U.S. House of Representatives Judiciary Committee, April 29, 1996.

The problem is that medical science has conquered the gentle and peaceful deaths and left the humiliating and agonizing to run their relentless downhill course. And it forces some to suffer through a slow and agonizing death that contradicts the very meaning and fabric of their lives.

By training I am a nurse, physician assistant, and attorney at law. I appear today in my role as a Chief Petitioner of Oregon's Death with Dignity Act, which was passed by citizens' initiative in November 1994. The Act creates a safe harbor in Oregon's assisted suicide laws for an attending physician to provide a prescription for lethal medication, upon repeated voluntary and informed requests from a competent, adult, terminally ill patient. The patient may then obtain the means for a humane and dignified death at the time of his or her own choosing. The Act imposes numerous safeguards, such as repeated written and oral requests, second medical opinions, waiting periods, and consultation regarding comfort care, hospice and pain control. It also provides for documentation by the attending physician and oversight by the State Health Division.

DEATH WITH DIGNITY

The movement for Oregon's Death with Dignity Act began with Oregon families that had struggled through prolonged and painful deaths and resolved to change the law. Elvin Sinnard's wife Sarah suffered with a terminal heart condition that brought excruciating pain with any activity, including reading and talking. She reached her decision in consultation with her family and minister, stockpiled medication and learned how to apply a plastic bag. Heartened by her empowerment, she continued to live for a number of months, but gradually her suffering became too great to bear. When the day of her decision arrived, she carefully constructed an alibi for her husband and instructed him to go where he would be seen, not to return for a stated number of hours. When he returned she indeed was "at peace" but his grief was intensified at his inability to be with her when she died. In spite of Sarah's precautions, Elvin was still subjected to a criminal investigation. The house was searched and articles confiscated, including Sarah's farewell letters to her family. Elvin declared, "This isn't right," and formed an organization called Oregon Right to Die, which met in his basement.

SLOW SUFFERING

Patty Rosen's daughter Jody was dying of bone cancer. All the narcotics doctors could provide didn't dull her pain and Jody pleaded with her mother, a nurse, to help her die. The day Patty finally agreed was a happy one for Jody, but complying with her request was not easy because of the drug tolerance that had developed over the previous weeks. Patty eventually succeeded, and lay next to her daughter as she died in her bed.

The problem is that medical science has conquered the gentle and peaceful deaths and left the humiliating and agonizing to run their relentless downhill course. The suffering of these individuals is not trivial, and it is not addressed by anything medical science has to offer. Faced with this dilemma, the problem for many is that the law turns loving families into criminals. It separates loved ones at the end, when it is most important to be close. It encourages patients to choose violent and premature deaths while they still have the strength to act. And it forces some to suffer through a slow and agonizing death that contradicts the very meaning and fabric of their lives.

A SPECTRUM OF SUPPORT

In Oregon the Death with Dignity Act received wide support across genders, ages, and political philosophies. The state Democratic party, ACLU and local National Organization of Women supported the Act as a compassionate response to the dilemma many find themselves in at the end of their lives. But our most vocal support and largest contributions came from people who describe themselves as politically very conservative. They resent a government that interferes in an intensely personal, private decision, and restricts their individual liberty. Many who would oppose a woman's abortion option on the grounds that there is another life to be considered, see no such moral issue in assisted death for terminally ill adults.

LEGITIMIZING SUPPORTERS

During our campaign we argued that physicians already assist their patients with death in hidden and unstated ways. The initiative would merely bring covert, surreptitious activity into the open and add safeguards. Recent scientific evidence confirms this belief. The *New England Journal of Medicine* published a 1995 survey of Oregon physicians, in which 21% said they had been asked for a prescription for a lethal dose of medication within the preceding year. Seven percent (7%) stated they had written such a prescription prior to passage of the Act, and most of these stated their patients had taken the medication. A survey of Washington State physicians published in the *Journal of the American Medical Association* revealed that 26% of physicians have been asked at least once for a lethal prescription or euthanasia. One hundred forty-seven physicians provided 207 case descriptions of patients who made requests. The physician provided lethal prescriptions to 38 (24%) of those requesting them and 21 patients (55%) took the medication and died. Fifteen patients (39%) did not use their prescriptions.

Physicians who respond to such requests do so without guidelines, without consultation with their peers, and without referral for second opinion. Improvement in these professional practices is one of the chief salutary effects of decriminalization. With open discussion of symptoms and options comes improvement in care. Since passage of the Death with Dignity Act, palliative care has received greatly increased attention in Oregon's medical community and referral to hospice has increased 20%. Dying individuals and their families are relieved of their burden of secrecy, isolation and fear of prosecution.

THE NECESSITY OF DECRIMINALIZATION

Incredibly, some would contend that covert, illegal assistance is preferable to decriminalization. As a citizen and attorney I believe in an ordered society and I could not accept for a stated policy to wink at the law. When we know that certain rare and desperate cases call for a compassionate response in the form of assisted death, our democratic heritage demands that the law be consistent with that knowledge. Perhaps this is uniquely American, but it is how we govern with integrity to retain the consent of the governed.

I believe that one reason people like Sarah, or Jody, or Francois Mitterand choose a hastened death, is because they believe the circumstances of their deaths are very important to the meaning, the story, even the sanctity of their lives. There is something about facing death with courage and grace, with senses intact, that serves their most cherished values and spiritual needs.

READING

7

DECRIMINALIZATION IS A VIOLATION

Robert J. Castagna

Robert J. Castagna is general council and executive director of the Oregon Catholic Conference. Representing 300,000 Roman Catholics in Oregon, the Conference discusses and formulates public policy positions in light of Church teaching. The Conference was one of the most vocal opponents to Oregon Ballot Measure 16.

■ **POINTS TO CONSIDER**

1. According to Castagna, what interest does the Roman Catholic Church have in the assisted suicide debate?

2. Summarize the history of decriminalization of assisted suicide, according to the Catholic Conference.

3. Evaluate the author's claim that Oregon Ballot Measure 16 "sanitizes" euthanasia.

4. Discuss at least two ways in which the Oregon Law may conflict with federal law, according to the article.

Excerpted from the testimony of Robert J. Castagna before the Subcommittee on Health and the Environment of the U.S. House of Representatives Commerce Committee, March 6, 1997.

Oregon stands at the threshold of an unwise and dangerous public policy which will pay for a lethal overdose of drugs for terminally ill persons, but not provide benefits for drugs which keep people alive.

The Conference has particular interest in the issue of physician-assisted suicide. Catholic Church teaching is well articulated on this issue: the Church supports the dignity of the individual throughout life's journey from conception until natural death. Accordingly, the Conference opposes physician-assisted suicide and has been engaged significantly in the public debate in Oregon on this issue.

BRIEF HISTORY OF PHYSICIAN-ASSISTED SUICIDE ON THE WEST COAST

Ballot Measure 16 is the first legislation to be adopted anywhere in the world decriminalizing physician-assisted suicide. On Election Day, November 8, 1994, Ballot Measure 16 was approved narrowly by Oregon's voters 51%-49%. The Ballot Measure 16 official vote, as published by Oregon's Secretary of State in the 1995-96 Oregon Blue Book, was 627,980 "Yes" votes and 596, 018 "No" votes, a difference of 31,962 votes. In Multnomah County, the state's most populous county, the margin in favor of Measure 16 was 33,413 votes. Outside Multnomah County, the opposition prevailed by a margin of 1,451 votes. The opponents prevailed in 21 of Oregon's 36 counties. A change of 16,000 votes from "Yes" to "No" would have changed the outcome of the election.

Since 1988 the issues of physician-assisted suicide and euthanasia have been prominent in Oregon. Having failed to qualify a proposition for California's statewide ballot in 1988, the Hemlock Society moved its national headquarters to Eugene, Oregon, in August 1988. In June 1989, while the Oregon Legislative Assembly was considering the adoption of power-of-attorney for health care legislation, the proponents of assisted suicide and euthanasia filed an initiative petition with the Oregon Secretary of State. The operative term "aid-in-dying" would have permitted the administration of a lethal injection by a physician.

In the face of a ballot-title challenge before the Oregon Supreme Court, as provided under Oregon's initiative election law, the petitioners withdrew their initiative. They announced they had secured the commitment of a state legislator who promised to introduce similar legislation in 1991 during the next regularly scheduled session of the Oregon Legislative Assembly.

In 1990 the proponents moved their efforts north to Washington State and filed an initiative to the Washington Legislature again permitting "aid-in-dying" and the administration of the lethal injection by a physician. The 1991 Washington State Legislature did not adopt the measure. Instead, Initiative 119 was placed on the November 1991 statewide ballot where it was defeated 54%-46%.

In Oregon in 1991, S.B. 1141 was introduced by four state legislators. The bill received one hearing and died in committee. Once again, "aid-in-dying" was the cornerstone euphemism permitting a physician to administer a lethal injection.

In 1992, the proponents' focus shifted once again to California in the form of Proposition 161. "Aid in dying" would have allowed the administration of the lethal injection by a physician. Proposition 161 was defeated by the same margin as the vote in Washington State, 54%-46%.

BALLOT MEASURE 16

Having learned from their defeats in Washington State (1991) and California (1992), the proponents of physician-assisted suicide and euthanasia dropped the lethal injection in their return to Oregon in 1994. In its pertinent section, Ballot Measure 16 states:

"Nothing in this Act shall be construed to authorize a physician or any other person to end a patient's life by lethal injection, mercy killing or active euthanasia. Actions taken in accordance with this Act shall not, for any purpose, constitute suicide, assisted suicide, mercy killing or homicide, under the law." (Section 3.14)

Ballot Measure 16 was the sanitized version of the euthanasia movement's public policy efforts. The doctors would not be directly involved in killing the patient. Instead, under the measure's terms, an adult "...may make a written request for medication for the purpose of ending his or her life in a humane and dignified manner in accordance with this Act." (Section 2.01)

Cartoon by Richard Wright.

Additionally, Ballot Measure 16's express language plays havoc with commonly understood words and definitions, e.g., suicide, assisted suicide, mercy killing and homicide.

SUBSIDIZING DEATH

On December 6, 1994, The *Statesman-Journal* ran a story under the headline "State Could Cover Assisted Suicide." The article included the following statement: "Jean Thorne, the state's Medicaid director, said physician-assisted suicide, if done according to the law, would be covered under a part of the Oregon Health Plan called comfort care."

On Sunday, February 16, 1997, The *New York Times* ran a front page story under the headline "Expense Means Many Can't Get Drugs for AIDS." The story stated: "The AIDS drug assistance programs in Arkansas, Nevada, South Dakota and Oregon do not cover any of the protease inhibitors, which block reproduction of the AIDS virus. Covering such drugs 'would blow our budget out of the water,' said Lisa McAuliffe, coordinator of the Oregon program."

Oregon stands at the threshold of an unwise and dangerous public policy which will pay for a lethal overdose of drugs for terminally ill persons, but not provide benefits for drugs which block reproduction of the AIDS virus to keep people alive. Public policy which pays for death and refuses to pay for life is morally bankrupt.

On December 4, 1994, The *Oregonian* reported on the study by a euthanasia doctor from the Netherlands, Dr. Pieter Admiraal:

> "He said it chronicled more than 200 patients over a four-year period and quantified what Dutch physicians have known for years: Drugs work slowly for some people.
>
> The study showed that while 75 percent of the patients die within three hours, the remainder can last two days or longer. There is no way to predict who will die quickly and who will linger, Admiraal said.
>
> In the Netherlands, if a patient lingers, the physician often hastens death with a lethal injection. Here, doctors will not have that option."

The strategy to sanitize physician-assisted suicide by prohibiting lethal injection and by distancing doctors from the act of suicide may have worked in the campaign; but it produced a fundamentally and fatally flawed piece of legislation which, according to Admiraal's research, will not work immediately in 25 percent of the cases.

IN CONFLICT WITH FEDERAL LAW

Implementation of Ballot Measure 16 decriminalizing physician-assisted suicide may require the prescribing of barbiturates and other drugs for the intentional taking of human life – a purpose never approved by the Federal Food, Drug, and Cosmetic Act or the Controlled Substances Act.

Under the Religious Freedom Restoration Act (RFRA), a state may not substantially burden the exercise of religious freedom unless this is the most narrowly drawn means of serving a compelling state interest.

The Catholic Health Association (CHA) brief (filed in the Ninth U.S. Circuit Court of Appeals, 1995) says that even though Oregon's law "allows Catholic providers to transfer a patient

HISTORY LESSONS

The experience of Nazi Germany is relevant here, not because the advocates of assisted suicide are incipient fascists (they're not) but because of the historical fact that the Holocaust had its beginnings in the systematic elimination of Germans with disabilities....

Evan J. Kemp, Jr. "Could You Please Die Now?" **The Washington Post Weekly Edition.** January 13, 1997: 23.

rather than actually perform an assisted suicide, before the transfer, the facility must enable the suicide by creating the documentary record required by law to permit the last act in the sequence, the prescription of the fatal medication."

In a preliminary injunction against Oregon's Ballot Measure 16, U.S. District Court Judge Michael Hogan said questions have been raised as to whether a law selectively allowing assisted suicide for people with AIDS and other disabilities violates the federal Americans with Disabilities Act.

CONCLUSION

The British Parliament in a report on medical ethics wrote that "prohibition of intentional killing is the cornerstone of law and of social relationships." Ballot Measure 16 strikes a fundamental blow at the cornerstone of life in Oregon and the United States.

READING

8

THE FEDERAL GOVERNMENT WILL NOT PROSECUTE OREGON PHYSICIANS

Janet Reno

Janet Reno is the Attorney General of the United States for the Clinton Administration. The following is a response letter to U.S. House of Representatives Judiciary Chairperson Henry Hyde (R-IL).

■ POINTS TO CONSIDER

1. Why does the Attorney General write this letter to Chairperson Hyde?

2. Describe the "CSA."

3. Summarize Thomas Constantine's response to Congressperson Hyde's inquiry.

4. Contrast the Constantine and Reno responses to the question of DEA policy. How do they differ on the role of the federal government in the issue of Oregon's physician-assisted suicide law?

Excerpted from a letter from U.S. Attorney General Janet Reno to Congressperson Henry Hyde, Chairman of the House Judiciary Committee, June 5, 1998.

There is no evidence that Congress, in the Controlled Substances Act (CSA), intended to displace the state as the primary regulator of the medical profession, or to override a state's determination as to what constitutes legitimate medical practice.

This is in response to your request concerning the question as to whether the Department of Justice, through the Drug Enforcement Administration (DEA), may invoke the Controlled Substances Act (CSA), 21 U.S.C. §§ 801-971, to take adverse action against physicians who assist patients in ending their lives by prescribing controlled substances.

RE: OREGON LAW

The issue has arisen in the context of Oregon's Death with Dignity Act, Oreg. Rev. Stat. §§ 127.800-127.995, which permits physicians to assist competent, terminally ill patients in ending their lives in compliance with certain detailed procedures. The Department has reviewed the issue thoroughly and has concluded that adverse action against a physician who has assisted in a suicide in full compliance with the Oregon Act would not be authorized by the CSA.

The Oregon Act was approved by Oregon voters on November 8, 1994, and went into effect on October 27, 1997. The Act provides for a detailed procedure by which a mentally competent, terminally ill patient may request to end his or her life "in a humane and dignified manner," O.R.S. § 127.805. The procedure requires, for example, that the patient's competence and the voluntariness of the request be documented in writing and confirmed by two witnesses, that the patient's illness and competence and the voluntariness of the request be confirmed by a second physician, and that the physician and patient observe certain waiting periods. Once a request has been properly documented and the requisite waiting periods have expired, the patient's attending physician may prescribe, but not administer, medication to enable the patient to take his or her own life. As a matter of state law, physicians acting in accordance with the Oregon Act are immune from liability as well as any adverse disciplinary action for having rendered such assistance.

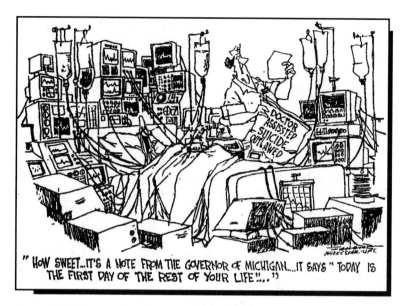

" HOW SWEET...IT'S A NOTE FROM THE GOVERNOR OF MICHIGAN....IT SAYS " TODAY IS
THE FIRST DAY OF THE REST OF YOUR LIFE"..."

Cartoon by Bill Schorr. Reprinted with permission, **UFS.**

REVERSAL OF CONSTANTINE

Prior to the Oregon Act's taking effect last year, you wrote to DEA Administrator Thomas Constantine seeking the DEA's view as to whether delivering, distributing, dispensing, prescribing, or administering a controlled substance with the intent of assisting in a suicide would violate the CSA, notwithstanding a state law such as the Oregon Act. In response, Administrator Constantine explained that "physician-assisted suicide would be a new and different application of the CSA," and that the determination whether to pursue adverse action under the CSA would first require "a medico-legal investigation" involving "state and local law enforcement agencies and prosecutors." He also stated, however, that "the activities that you described in your letter to us would be, in our opinion, a violation of the CSA." The Justice Department has conducted a thorough and careful review of the issue of whether the CSA authorizes adverse action against a physician who prescribes a controlled substance to assist in a suicide in compliance with Oregon law.

THE SCOPE OF THE LAW

The CSA is a complex regulatory scheme that controls the authorized distribution of scheduled drugs. Physicians, for example, are authorized to prescribe and distribute scheduled drugs

63

only pursuant to their registration with DEA, and the unauthorized distribution of drugs is generally subject to criminal and administrative action. The relevant provisions of the CSA provide criminal penalties for physicians who dispense controlled substances beyond "the course of professional practice," 21 U.S.C. § 802(21), id. § 841(b), and provide for revocation of the DEA drug registrations of physicians who have engaged either in such criminal conduct or in other "conduct which may threaten the public health and safety," id. § 823(f).

The CSA was intended to keep legally available controlled substances within lawful channels of distribution and use. It sought to prevent both the trafficking in these substances for unauthorized purposes and drug abuse. The particular drug abuse that Congress intended to prevent was that deriving from the drug's "stimulant, depressant, or hallucinogenic effect on the central nervous system," 21 U.S.C. § 811(f).

STATE, LAW AND MORALITY

There is no evidence that Congress, in the CSA, intended to displace the state as the primary regulator of the medical profession, or to override a state's determination as to what constitutes legitimate medical practice in the absence of a federal law prohibiting that practice. Indeed, the CSA is essentially silent with regard to regulating the practice of medicine that involves legally available drugs (except for certain specific regulations dealing with the treatment of addicts).

Even more fundamentally, there is no evidence that Congress, in the CSA, intended to assign DEA the novel role of resolving the "earnest and profound debate about the morality, legality, and practicality of physician-assisted suicide," Washington v. Glucksberg, 117 S. Ct. 2258, 2275 (1997), simply because that procedure involves the use of controlled substances. If Congress had assigned DEA this role under the CSA, it would ultimately be DEA's task to determine whether assistance in the commission of a suicide, in compliance with a state law specifically permitting and regulating such assistance, nevertheless falls outside the legitimate practice of medicine and is inconsistent with the public interest. These questions, however, are not susceptible of scientific or factual resolution, but rather are fundamental questions of morality and public policy. Such a mission falls well beyond the purpose of the CSA.

THE DEA RESPONDS TO HYDE

We are persuaded that delivering, dispensing or prescribing a controlled substance with the intent of assisting a suicide would not be under any current definition a "legitimate medical purpose." As a result, the activities that you described in your letter to us would be, in our opinion, a violation of the CSA.

Excerpted from a letter from Thomas A. Constantine, Administrator of the Drug Enforcement Agency (DEA) to Henry Hyde, Chairperson of the U.S. House of Representatives Judiciary Committee, November 5, 1997.

HONORING OREGON LAW

The State of Oregon has reached the considered judgment that physician-assisted suicide should be authorized under narrow conditions and in compliance with certain detailed procedures. Under these circumstances, we have concluded that the CSA does not authorize DEA to prosecute, or to revoke the DEA registration of, a physician who has assisted in a suicide in compliance with Oregon law. We emphasize that our conclusion is limited to these particular circumstances. Adverse action under the CSA may well be warranted in other circumstances: for example, where a physician assists in a suicide in a state that has not authorized the practice under any conditions, or where a physician fails to comply with state procedures in doing so.

CONCLUSION

Finally, notwithstanding our interpretation of the CSA as it applies to the Oregon Act, it is important to underscore that the President continues to maintain his longstanding position against assisted suicide and any federal support for that procedure. This position was recently codified when he signed the Assisted Suicide Funding Restriction Act last year. While states ordinarily have primary responsibility for regulating physicians, the President and the Administration nonetheless remain open to working with you and other interested members of Congress on this complex but extremely important issue.

FEDERAL ACTION IS NEEDED

Burke J. Balch

Burke J. Balch is the director of the National Right to Life Committee. The National Right to Life News *is published by the National Right to Life Committee, a nonprofit organization which actively opposes physician-assisted suicide and abortion. Founded in 1973, it is the largest pro-life group in the nation.*

■ **POINTS TO CONSIDER**

1. Why are Congresspersons Hyde and Oberstar introducing legislation? How does this relate to the Oregon Law?

2. Explain the "inconsistency" on the part of physician-assisted suicide advocates, according to Balch.

3. According to the reading, how would the potential federal action affect doctors in their mission of pain relief?

4. Summarize, then discuss, the author's response to the contention that the U.S. needs to bring the practice of euthanasia out in the open.

Excerpted from Balch, Burke. "House Votes on Pivotal Euthanasia Law Expected Soon," **National Right to Life News**. July 8, 1998: 1, 10, 15. Reprinted by permission, National Right to Life Committee, Inc.

Ironically, some pro-euthanasia groups raising the "states' rights" issue are the same people who in 1997 brought suits to the Supreme Court that unsuccessfully sought to take away states' rights to prevent assisting suicide.

On Tuesday, July 13, 1998, the House Judiciary Subcommittee on the Constitution, chaired by representative Charles T. Canady (R-FL), held hearings on the Lethal Drug Abuse Prevention Act of 1998, H.R. 4006. The bill, sponsored by Henry Hyde (R-IL) and James Oberstar (D-MN), would prevent the use of federally controlled narcotics and other dangerous drugs to assist suicide....

SPREAD OF EUTHANASIA

"This is an extraordinarily important opportunity to prevent the spread of euthanasia," said National Right to Life Committee (NRLC) Executive Director David N. O'Steen, Ph.D. "The next few weeks will see a critical debate on whether America chooses the road of life or death for older people, people with disabilities, and those most vulnerable in our society."

Following is a question and answer dialogue summarizing the facts and arguments relevant to the bill....

NEED AND PURPOSE

Q. What would the Legal Drug Abuse Prevention Act of 1998 do?

A. Federal law and regulations now generally prohibit the distribution of certain narcotics and other dangerous drugs unless a doctor who has been granted a special "registration" by the federal Drug Enforcement Administration (DEA) prescribes them for a legitimate medical purpose. The bill would prevent doctors from using this federally conferred authority to obtain controlled substances in order to kill their patients. It would authorize revoking the DEA registration of doctors who use it to prescribe drugs to assist suicide.

Q. Why is the Lethal Drug Abuse Prevention Act of 1998 needed?

A. By referendum Oregon has adopted a law legalizing certain cases of assisted suicide, which is now in force. On November 5,

1997, the DEA ruled that under the current language of the federal Controlled Substances Act doctors could not use their DEA registrations to prescribe federally controlled substances in order to assist suicide. However, on June 5, 1998, Attorney General Janet Reno reversed this ruling, instead authorizing the use of federally controlled substances to kill patients to the extent such killing is permitted by state law. The bill is needed to reinstate what in the opinion of the professionals at the DEA is current law. Otherwise, the federal government will be affirmatively facilitating euthanasia by specifically authorizing the use of federally controlled drugs to assist suicide.

Q. Where does the public stand?

A. By a margin of more than two to one (65% to 29%), Americans oppose allowing the use of "federally controlled drugs for the purpose of assisted suicide and euthanasia" (Wirthlin Worldwide poll, March 7-9, 1998; 4.3% margin of error).

FEDERAL CONTRIBUTION

Q. Has Congress already spoken on the issue of federal government involvement in assisting suicide?

A. Yes. Congress passed (by 99-0 in the Senate and 398-16 in the House) and President Clinton signed the Assisted Suicide Funding Restriction Act of 1997, which prevents the use of federal funds or facilities to assist suicide or for euthanasia. The Lethal Drug Abuse Prevention Act of 1998 is a logical application of the intent of that act to avoid federal facilitation of assisting suicide through the use of federally controlled drugs.

Q. Would the Lethal Drug Abuse Prevention Act of 1998 infringe on states' rights?

A. The Controlled Substances Act was adopted almost 30 years ago (in 1970) and strengthened in 1984 because drug abuse was seen as a national problem requiring regulation beyond the state level. So when California and Arizona by referendum legalized the use of medicinal marijuana, the Justice Department acted to secure injunctions against marijuana dispensers, successfully persuading the court that regardless of state law, the distribution of marijuana for any purpose still violated federal law.

Enforcement of the Lethal Drug Abuse Prevention Act would neither nullify nor change the laws of Oregon or any other state. It is an established legal principle that the laws of one state cannot nullify federal law....

Ironically, some pro-euthanasia groups raising the "states' rights" issue, like Compassion in Dying, are the same people who in 1997 brought suits to the Supreme Court that unsuccessfully sought to take away states' rights to prevent assisting suicide.

PROMOTING PAIN RELIEF

Q. Would the Lethal Drug Abuse Prevention Act of 1998 deter doctors from prescribing the large doses of controlled substances sometimes necessary to control pain for fear that they could be accused of assisting suicide?

A. On the contrary, the Lethal Drug Abuse Prevention Act would diminish the danger of deterring adequate pain relief that may be present under current law.

To promote the provision of good pain relief, the bill amends the current Controlled Substances Act by adding new language making a distinction between providing a controlled substance for the purpose of pain relief, even with the risk of death – which the bill specifically permits – and providing a controlled substance for the purpose of causing death, for which a doctor's DEA registration may be revoked. To reassure physicians that they can safely prescribe controlled substances for pain relief, the bill provides that a doctor threatened with suspension or revocation may demand a hearing before a Medical Review Board on Pain Relief composed of clinical experts in pain management, who will make findings as to whether any disputed prescription was an appropriate means to relieve pain as opposed to an act of euthanasia.

Under the Attorney General's June 5, 1998, ruling, the DEA can revoke a doctor's DEA registration for assisting a suicide contrary to state law: At present, therefore, the Controlled Substances Act will be enforced against assisting suicide in almost all of the states, but without any explicit protection or safeguards for doctors prescribing controlled substances for pain management. Even in Oregon, it will be enforced against a doctor who assists any suicide that does not fall under the circumstances in which the state has legalized assisting suicide.

Thus, the bill will not only reinstate the DEA's position that federally controlled drugs cannot be used to assist suicide – an

EUTHANIZING BABIES

It has been estimated that, in the Netherlands, the lives of ten severely handicapped neonates are actively terminated each year. Yet, there is still no clear consensus about the morality of actively ending the lives of severely disabled newborns who – even after the withdrawal of medical treatment – continue to live and to suffer. Some physicians believe that the lives of these babies should be actively terminated; others do not....

Arlene Judith Klotzko. "A Report from the Netherlands: What Kind of Life? What Kind of Death?" **Bioethics**. January 1997: 24.

affirmation of the *status quo* before the Reno decision – but also remove a perceived barrier to the provision of adequate pain relief.

PROTECTING THE VULNERABLE

Q. How do you answer this argument: "Doctors assist people's suicides everyday. It's going to happen whether it's legal or illegal. But if it is legal then it can be regulated. We need more Oregons, not more Kevorkians. We need to bring this practice out of the darkness and into the light."

A. First, laws that protect the vulnerable against assisted suicide are effective. A study published in the April 23, 1998, *New England Journal of Medicine* showed that while 36% of doctors would be willing to write lethal prescriptions if assisting suicide were legal, only 11% are willing to do so while it is against the law. Currently, while 18.3% of doctors have been asked to assist suicide with a lethal prescription, only 3.3% have done so. The laws against euthanasia are effectively deterring over two-thirds of doctors who otherwise might assist suicide.

Second, if some doctors are now willing to violate laws that prohibit assisting suicide, why should we suppose those same doctors would not be equally ready to violate laws regulating it whenever they think the regulations impose limits or procedures with which they disagree?

The answer to current violations of laws protecting against euthanasia is to pass more effective euthanasia laws and to better enforce those we now have, not to legalize it....

COMPARING CULTURAL VALUES

This activity may be used as an individualized study guide for students in libraries and resource centers or as a discussion catalyst in small group and classroom discussions.

A. **Conflicting Social Values**

Examine carefully the three value systems and identify the differences and common grounds.

Moral System One:	Moral System Two:	Moral System Three:
1. Life begins at conception and should be protected, no matter in what state, until natural death. The option for physician-assisted suicide is not part of my moral beliefs. 2. My moral system is set by God and is clearly and literally outlined by scriptures.	1. Life begins at birth and should be protected under most circumstances until natural death. Physician-assisted suicide should be allowed, but extremely limited. 2. Faith is important in my life and largely shapes my moral views. Since the message of scripture is sometimes unclear, I analyze scripture in light of changing human needs.	1. I believe life begins at conception, but that the public debate on the subject is irrelevant. Law must protect individuals' right to do whatever they wish with their bodies. 2. I am an agnostic. My moral system is primarily shaped by the physical world around me.

B. Points to Consider

Working as individuals or in small discussion groups, read through the following statements and evaluate each one as indicated.

• **Mark (A)** for any statement with which you agree.

• **Mark (D)** for any statement with which you disagree.

• **Mark (N)** for any statement you are not sure about.

_____1. Moral System One offers the best way to protect life.

_____2. Moral System Two offers the best way to value life.

_____3. Moral System Three offers the best way to respect life.

_____4. The problem with Moral System One is that it does not take into consideration individual circumstances and differing beliefs.

_____5. The problem with Moral System Two is that it does not safeguard vulnerable people.

_____6. The problem with Moral System Three is that it values the individual too much before the good of society.

C. Reaching an Understanding

Craft a short essay which describes your values system, its foundation, and how it informs you on the issue of physician-assisted suicide. Share this with your class discussion group.

CHAPTER 3

INDIVIDUAL AND STATE: ASSISTED SUICIDE IN THE U.S. COURTS

CITIZENS MAY EXERT THEIR CONSTITUTIONALLY PROTECTED RIGHT TO DIE

Stephen Reinhardt

Stephen Reinhardt is a Circuit Judge of the Ninth U.S. Circuit Court of Appeals of Northern California. In January 1994, four Washington State physicians, along with three terminally ill patients, sought a declaration in Federal District Court that a Washington State statute prohibiting assisted suicide is unconstitutional. The District Court agreed with the petitioners citing that the statute violated the Equal Protection Clause and the liberty interest of the terminally ill protected under the Fourteenth Amendment. A panel of three of the Court of Appeals for the Ninth Circuit reversed the District Court Decision. However, the Ninth Circuit Court of Appeals reheard the case, en banc, *and reversed the panel's decision, affirming the decision of the District Court, that the Washington statute is unconstitutional. Judge Reinhardt delivered the opinion of the court.*

■ POINTS TO CONSIDER

1. Discuss the content of the Washington State law in question. What is the Ninth U.S. Circuit Court of Appeals ruling of its constitutionality and upon what grounds does the court make its ruling?
2. Why does the court create a link between abortion and assisted suicide?
3. What role does the state have in overseeing assisted suicide, according to the court?
4. Discuss the court's view of history, common law tradition and legal statute in deciding this case.

Excerpted from the opinion of the Ninth U.S. Circuit Court of Appeals in Compassion in Dying v. Washington (1995) 79 F3d 790.

We hold that insofar as the Washington statute prohibits physicians from prescribing life-ending medication for use by terminally ill, competent adults who wish to hasten their own deaths, it violates the Due Process Clause of the Fourteenth Amendment.

Today, we are required to decide whether a person who is terminally ill has a constitutionally protected liberty interest in hastening what might otherwise be a protracted, undignified, and extremely painful death. If such an interest exists, we must next decide whether or not the State of Washington may constitutionally restrict its exercise by banning a form of medical assistance that is frequently requested by terminally ill people who wish to die. We first conclude that there is a constitutionally protected liberty interest in determining the time and manner of one's own death, an interest that must be weighed against the state's legitimate and countervailing interests, especially those that relate to the preservation of human life. After balancing the competing interests, we conclude by answering the narrow question before us: We hold that insofar as the Washington statute prohibits physicians from prescribing life-ending medication for use by terminally ill, competent adults who wish to hasten their own deaths, it violates the Due Process Clause of the Fourteenth Amendment.

Under the Washington statute, aiding a person who wishes to end his life constitutes a criminal act and subjects the aider to the possibility of a lengthy term of imprisonment, even if the recipient of the aid is a terminally ill, competent adult and the aider is a licensed physician who is providing medical assistance at the request of the patient.

DUE PROCESS VIOLATION

The full scope of the liberty guaranteed by the Due Process Clause cannot be found in or limited by the precise terms of the specific guarantees elsewhere in the Constitution. This "liberty" is not a series of isolated points picked out in terms of the taking of property; the freedom of speech, press, and religion; the right to keep and bear arms; the freedom from unreasonable searches and seizures; and so on. It is a rational continuum which, broadly speaking, includes a freedom from all substantial arbitrary impositions and purposeless restraints, ... and which also recognizes, what a reasonable and sensitive judgment must, that certain interests require particularly careful scrutiny of the stated needs asserted to justify their abridgment.

LIBERTY INTEREST

In examining whether a liberty interest exists in determining the time and manner of one's death, we begin with the compelling similarities between right-to-die cases and abortion cases. In the former as in the latter, the relative strength of the competing interests changes as physical, medical, or related circumstances vary. In right-to-die cases the outcome of the balancing test may differ at different points along the life cycle as a person's physical or medical condition deteriorates, just as in abortion cases the permissibility of restrictive state legislation may vary with the progression of the pregnancy. Equally important, both types of cases raise issues of life and death, and both arouse similar religious and moral concerns.

Both also present basic questions about an individual's right of choice.

Historical evidence shows that both abortion and assisted suicide were for many years condemned, but that the efforts to prevent people from engaging in the condemned conduct were always at most only partially successful. Even when prohibited, abortions and assisted suicides flourished in back alleys, in small street-side clinics, and in the privacy of the bedroom. Deprived of the right to medical assistance, many pregnant women and terminally ill adults ultimately took matters into their own hands, often with tragic consequences.

MORE PRECISE TERMINOLOGY

While some people refer to the liberty interest implicated in right-to-die cases as a liberty interest in committing suicide, we do not describe it that way. We use the broader and more accurate terms, "the right to die," "determining the time and manner of one's death," and "hastening one's death" for an important reason. The liberty interest we examine encompasses a whole range of acts that are generally not considered to constitute "suicide." Included within the liberty interest we examine, is for example, the act of refusing or terminating unwanted medical treatment. A competent adult has a liberty interest in refusing to be connected to a respirator or in being disconnected from one, even if he is

76

terminally ill and cannot live without mechanical assistance. The law does not classify the death of a patient that results from the granting of his wish to decline or discontinue treatment as "suicide." Nor does the law label the acts of those who help the patient carry out that wish, whether by physically disconnecting the respirator or by removing an intravenous tube, as assistance in suicide. Accordingly, we believe that the broader terms – "the right to die," "controlling the time and manner of one's death," and "hastening one's death" – more accurately describe the liberty interest at issue here. Moreover, we have serious doubts that the terms "suicide" and "assisted suicide" are appropriate legal descriptions of the specific conduct at issue here.

HISTORY AS GUIDE

Were history our sole guide, the Virginia anti-miscegenation statute that the Court unanimously overturned in *Loving v. Virginia*, 388 U.S. 1 (1967), as violative of substantive due process and the Equal Protection Clause, would still be in force because such anti-miscegenation laws were commonplace both when the United States was founded and when the Fourteenth Amendment was adopted.

Indeed, if historical evidence of accepted practices at the time the Fourteenth Amendment was enacted were dispositive, the Court would not only have decided *Loving* differently, but it would not have held that women have a right to have an abortion. As the dissent pointed out in *Roe*, more than three-quarters of the existing states (at least 28 out of 37 states), as well as eight territorial legislatures restricted or prohibited abortions in 1868 when the Fourteenth Amendment was adopted. *Roe*, 410 U.S. at 175-76.

SUICIDE IN HISTORY

The majority of states have not criminalized suicide or attempted suicide since the turn of the century. The New Jersey Supreme Court declared in 1901 that since suicide was not punishable it should not be considered a crime. "All will admit that in some cases it is ethically defensible," the court said, as when a woman kills herself to escape being raped or "when a man curtails weeks or months of agony of an incurable disease." Today, no state has a statute prohibiting suicide or attempted suicide; nor has any state had such a statute for at least ten years. A majority of states do, however, still have laws on the books against assisting suicide.

CURRENT SOCIETAL ATTITUDES

Clearly the absence of a criminal sanction alone does not show societal approbation of a practice. Nor is there any evidence that Americans approve of suicide in general. In recent years, however, there has been increasingly widespread support for allowing the terminally ill to hasten their deaths and avoid painful, undignified, and inhumane endings to their lives. Most Americans simply do not appear to view such acts as constituting suicide, and there is much support in reason for that conclusion.

Just as the mere absence of criminal statutes prohibiting suicide or attempted suicide does not indicate societal approval so the mere presence of statutes criminalizing assisting in a suicide does not necessarily indicate societal disapproval. That is especially true when such laws are seldom, if ever, enforced. There is no reported American case of criminal punishment being meted out to a doctor for helping a patient hasten his own death. The lack of enforcement of statutes prohibiting assisting a mentally competent, terminally ill adult to end his own life would appear to reflect widespread societal disaffection with such laws.

Our attitudes toward suicide of the type at issue in this case are better understood in light of our unwritten history and of technological developments. Running beneath the official history of legal condemnation of physician-assisted suicide is a strong undercurrent of a time-honored but hidden practice of physicians helping terminally ill patients to hasten their deaths. According to a survey by the American Society of Internal Medicine, one doctor in five said he had assisted in a patient's suicide. Accounts of doctors who have helped their patients end their lives have appeared both in professional journals and in the daily press.

PERSONAL DIGNITY

Like the decision of whether or not to have an abortion, the decision how and when to die is one of "the most intimate and personal choices a person may make in a lifetime," a choice "central to personal dignity and autonomy." A competent terminally ill adult, having lived nearly the full measure of his life, has a strong liberty interest in choosing a dignified and humane death rather than being reduced at the end of his existence to a childlike state of helplessness, diapered, sedated, incontinent. How a person dies not only determines the nature of the final period of his existence, but in many cases, the enduring memories held by those who love him.

PRESERVING LIFE

Our conclusion that there is a liberty interest in determining the time and manner of one's death does not mean that there is a concomitant right to exercise that interest in all circumstances or to do so free from state regulation. To the contrary, we explicitly recognize that some prohibitory and regulatory state action is fully consistent with constitutional principles.

In short, finding a liberty interest constitutes a critical first step toward answering the question before us. The determination that must now be made is whether the state's attempt to curtail the exercise of that interest is constitutionally justified.

The state may assert an unqualified interest in preserving life in general. As the Court said in *Cruzan*, "we think a State may properly decline to make judgments about the 'quality' of life that a particular individual may enjoy, and simply assert an unqualified interest in the preservation of human life...." Thus, the state may assert its interest in preserving life in all cases, including those of terminally ill, competent adults who wish to hasten their deaths.

DIMINISHED STATE INTERESTS

Although the state's interest in preserving life may be unqualified, and may be asserted regardless of the quality of the life or lives at issue, that interest is not always controlling. Nor is it of the same strength in each case. To the contrary, its strength is dependent on relevant circumstances, including the medical condition and the wishes of the person whose life is at stake.

Not only does Washington law acknowledge that terminally ill and permanently unconscious adults have a right to refuse life-sustaining treatment, the statute includes specific legislative findings that appear to recognize that a due process liberty interest underlies that right.

As the laws in state after state demonstrate, even though the protection of life is one of the state's most important functions, the state's interest is dramatically diminished if the person it seeks to protect is terminally ill or permanently comatose and has expressed a wish that he be permitted to die without further medical treatment (or if a duly appointed representative has done so on his behalf).

Step by step, the state has acknowledged that terminally ill persons are entitled in a whole variety of circumstances to hasten their deaths, and that in such cases their physicians may assist in the process.

Today, many states also allow the terminally ill to order their physicians to discontinue not just traditional medical treatment but the artificial provision of life-sustaining food and water, thus permitting the patients to die by self-starvation. Equally important, today, doctors are generally permitted to administer death-inducing medication, as long as they can point to a concomitant pain-relieving purpose.

CONCLUSION

Some argue strongly that decisions regarding matters affecting life or death should not be made by the courts. Essentially, we agree with that proposition. In this case, by permitting the individual to exercise the right to choose we are following the constitutional mandate to take such decisions out of the hands of the government, both state and federal, and to put them where they rightly belong, in the hands of the people.

READING

11

CITIZENS DO NOT HAVE A CONSTITUTIONALLY PROTECTED RIGHT TO DIE

William Rehnquist, Chief Justice

William Rehnquist is Chief Justice of the U.S. Supreme Court. He delivered the unanimous opinion of the Court in Washington v. Glucksberg. The decision of the court in June 1997 reversed an earlier decision of the Ninth Circuit Court of Appeals in Northern California (see previous reading). The Court ruled that a Washington statute prohibiting assisted suicide was consistent with the nation's legal tradition and not in violation of the Due Process Clause of the Fourteenth Amendment. Although the court did not recognize a constitutional "right to die," it left open the debate on the sanction of physician-assisted suicide to state legislatures.

■ POINTS TO CONSIDER

1. Summarize the various components that constitute the matter before the court.

2. Discuss the Common Law and legal history of assisted suicide in the U.S.

3. Describe the purpose of the Due Process Clause of the Fourteenth Amendment. How does this court feel about expanding due process?

4. Give at least three interests which the state has in prohibiting assisted suicide.

5. Contrast the ruling of the Supreme Court with that of the Ninth Circuit Court of Appeals (see previous reading) on the matter of Due Process.

Excerpted from the opinion of the United States Supreme Court in Washington v. Glucksberg (1997), 138 L Ed 2d 772, 117 S Ct 2258.

Throughout the Nation, Americans are engaged in an earnest and profound debate about the morality, legality, and practicality of physician-assisted suicide. Our holding permits this debate to continue, as it should in a democratic society.

The question presented in this case is whether Washington's prohibition against "causing" or "aiding" a suicide offends the Fourteenth Amendment to the United States Constitution. We hold that it does not.

THE WASHINGTON LAW

It has always been a crime to assist a suicide in the State of Washington. In 1854, Washington's first Territorial Legislature outlawed "assisting another in the commission of self-murder." Today, Washington law provides: "A person is guilty of promoting a suicide attempt when he knowingly causes or aids another person to attempt suicide." "Promoting a suicide attempt" is a felony, punishable by up to five years' imprisonment and up to a $10,000 fine. At the same time, Washington's Natural Death Act, enacted in 1979, states that the "withholding or withdrawal of life-sustaining treatment" at a patient's direction "shall not, for any purpose, constitute a suicide."

In January 1994, respondents, along with three gravely ill, pseudonymous plaintiffs who have since died and Compassion in Dying, a nonprofit organization that counsels people considering physician-assisted suicide, sued in the United States District Court, seeking a declaration that Washington Rev. Code 9A.36.060(1) (1994) is, on its face, unconstitutional.

HISTORY, TRADITION

We begin, as we do in all due-process cases, by examining our Nation's history, legal traditions, and practices. See *Planned Parenthood of Southeastern Pennsylvania v. Casey; Cruzan v. Director, Missouri Dept. of Health; Moore v. East Cleveland.* In almost every state – indeed, in almost every western democracy – it is a crime to assist a suicide. The states' assisted suicide bans are not innovations. Rather, they are longstanding expressions of the states' commitment to the protection and preservation of all human life. Indeed, opposition to and condemnation of suicide –

and, therefore, of assisting suicide – are consistent and enduring themes of our philosophical, legal, and cultural heritage.

More specifically, for over 700 years, the Anglo-American common-law tradition has punished or otherwise disapproved of both suicide and assisting suicide. In the 13th century, Henry de Bracton, one of the first legal treatise writers, observed that "just as a man may commit felony by slaying another so may he do so by slaying himself." The real and personal property of one who killed himself to avoid conviction and punishment for a crime were forfeit to the king. Centuries later, Sir William Blackstone emphasized that "the law has ... ranked suicide among the highest crimes," although, anticipating later developments, he conceded that the harsh and shameful punishments imposed for suicide "border a little upon severity."

Over time, however, the American colonies abolished these harsh common-law penalties. William Penn abandoned the criminal-forfeiture sanction in Pennsylvania in 1701, and the other colonies (and later, the other states) eventually followed this example.

That suicide remained a grievous, though nonfelonious, wrong is confirmed by the fact that colonial and early state legislatures and courts did not retreat from prohibiting assisting suicide. Zephaniah Swift, in his early 19th century treatise on the laws of Connecticut, stated that "if one counsels another to commit suicide, and the other by reason of the advice kills himself, the advisor is guilty of murder as principal."

The earliest American statute explicitly to outlaw assisting suicide was enacted in New York in 1828, and many of the new states and territories followed New York's example. By the time the Fourteenth Amendment was ratified, it was a crime in most states to assist a suicide. The Field Penal Code was adopted in the Dakota Territory in 1877, in New York in 1881, and its language served as a model for several other western states' statutes in the late 19th and early 20th centuries.

REAFFIRMING THE PROHIBITION

Though deeply rooted, the states' assisted suicide bans have in recent years been reexamined and, generally, reaffirmed. Because of advances in medicine and technology, Americans today are increasingly likely to die in institutions, from chronic illnesses.

Public concern and democratic action are therefore sharply focused on how best to protect dignity and independence at the end of life, with the result that there have been many significant changes in state laws and in the attitudes these laws reflect. Many states, for example, now permit "living wills," surrogate health-care decision making, and the withdrawal or refusal of life-sustaining medical treatment.

In 1991, Washington voters rejected a ballot initiative which, had it passed, would have permitted a form of physician-assisted suicide. Washington then added a provision to the Natural Death Act expressly excluding physician-assisted suicide.

Attitudes toward suicide itself have changed since Bracton, but our laws have consistently condemned, and continue to prohibit, assisting suicide. Despite changes in medical technology and notwithstanding an increased emphasis on the importance of end-of-life decision making, we have not retreated from this prohibition. Against this backdrop of history, tradition, and practice, we now turn to respondents' constitutional claim.

LIBERTY AND DUE PROCESS

The Due Process Clause guarantees more than fair process, and the "liberty" it protects includes more than the absence of physical restraint. (The Due Process Clause "protects individual liberty against 'certain government actions regardless of the fairness of the procedures used to implement them'," quoting *Daniels v. Williams*). The Clause also provides heightened protection against government interference with certain fundamental rights and liberty interests. We have also assumed, and strongly suggested, that the Due Process Clause protects the traditional right to refuse unwanted lifesaving medical treatment. But we "have always been reluctant to expand the concept of substantive due process because guideposts for responsible decisionmaking in this unchartered area are scarce and open-ended." *Collins v. Parker Heights*. By extending constitutional protection to an asserted right or liberty interest, we, to a great extent, place the matter outside the arena of public debate and legislative action. We must therefore "exercise the utmost care whenever we are asked to break new ground in this field," *ibid,* lest the liberty protected by the Due Process Clause be subtly transformed into the policy preferences of the members of this Court. *Moore.*

84

Turning to the claim at issue here, the Court of Appeals stated that "properly analyzed, the first issue to be resolved is whether there is a liberty interest in determining the time and manner of one's death," or, in other words, "is there a right to die?" The Washington statute at issue in this case prohibits "aiding another person to attempt suicide," and, thus, the question before us is whether the "liberty" specially protected by the Due Process Clause includes a right to commit suicide which itself includes a right to assistance in doing so.

We now inquire whether this asserted right has any place in our Nation's traditions. Here, as discussed above, we are confronted with a consistent and almost universal tradition that has long rejected the asserted right, and continues explicitly to reject it today, even for terminally ill, mentally competent adults. To hold for respondents, we would have to reverse centuries of legal doctrine and practice, and strike down the considered policy choice of almost every state.

The decision to commit suicide with the assistance of another may be just as personal and profound as the decision to refuse unwanted medical treatment, but it has never enjoyed similar legal protection. Indeed, the two acts are widely and reasonably regarded as quite distinct.

INTERESTS OF THE STATE

The history of the law's treatment of assisted suicide in this country has been and continues to be one of the rejection of nearly all efforts to permit it. That being the case, our decisions lead us to conclude that the asserted "right" to assistance in committing suicide is not a fundamental liberty interest protected by the Due Process Clause. The Constitution also requires, however, that Washington's assisted suicide ban be rationally related to legitimate government interests.

First, Washington has an "unqualified interest in the preservation of human life." *Cruzan.* The State's prohibition on assisted suicide, like all homicide laws, both reflects and advances its commitment to this interest.

Respondents admit that "the State has a real interest in preserving the lives of those who can still contribute to society and enjoy life." The Court of Appeals also recognized Washington's interest in protecting life, but held that the "weight" of this interest depends on the "medical condition and the wishes of the person whose life is at stake." Washington, however, has rejected this sliding-scale approach and, through its assisted suicide ban, insists that all persons' lives, from beginning to end, regardless of physical or mental condition, are under the full protection of the law.

The State has an interest in preventing suicide, and in studying, identifying, and treating its causes. Those who attempt suicide – terminally ill or not – often suffer from depression or other mental disorders. See New York Task Force (more than 95% of those who commit suicide had a major psychiatric illness at the time of death; among the terminally ill, uncontrolled pain is a "risk factor" because it contributes to depression).

The State also has an interest in protecting the integrity and ethics of the medical profession. In contrast to the Court of Appeals' conclusion that "the integrity of the medical profession would not be threatened in any way by physician-assisted suicide," the American Medical Association, like many other medical and physicians' groups, has concluded that "physician-assisted suicide is fundamentally incompatible with the physician's role as healer."

PROTECTING THE VULNERABLE

Next, the State has an interest in protecting vulnerable groups – including the poor, the elderly, and disabled persons – from abuse, neglect, and mistakes. The Court of Appeals dismissed the State's concern that disadvantaged persons might be pressured into physician-assisted suicide as "ludicrous on its face." We have recognized, however, the real risk of subtle coercion and undue influence in end-of-life situations. If physician-assisted suicide were permitted, many might resort to it to spare their families the substantial financial burden of end-of-life health-care costs.

The State's interest here goes beyond protecting the vulnerable from coercion; it extends to protecting disabled and terminally ill people from prejudice, negative and inaccurate stereotypes, and "societal indifference." 49F.3d, at 592. The State's assisted suicide ban reflects and reinforces its policy that the lives of terminally ill, disabled, and elderly people must be no less valued than the lives of the young and healthy, and that a seriously disabled person's suicidal impulses should be interpreted and treated the same way as anyone else's.

Finally, the State may fear that permitting assisted suicide will start it down the path to voluntary and perhaps even involuntary euthanasia. The Court of Appeals struck down Washington's assisted suicide ban only "as applied to competent, terminally ill adults who wish to hasten their deaths by obtaining medication prescribed by their doctors." Washington insists, however, that the impact of the court's decision will not and cannot be so limited. If suicide is protected as a matter of constitutional right, it is argued, "every man and woman in the United States must enjoy it."

CONTINUED DEBATE

We need not weigh exactingly the relative strengths of these various interests. They are unquestionably important and legitimate, and Washington's ban on assisted suicide is at least reasonably related to their promotion and protection. We therefore hold that Washington Rev. Code § 9A.36.060(1) (1994) does not violate the Fourteenth Amendment, either on its face or "as applied to competent, terminally ill adults who wish to hasten their deaths by obtaining medication prescribed by their doctors."

Throughout the Nation, Americans are engaged in an earnest and profound debate about the morality, legality, and practicality of physician-assisted suicide. Our holding permits this debate to continue, as it should in a democratic society. The decision of the *en banc* Court of Appeals is reversed, and the case is remanded for further proceedings consistent with this opinion.

It is so ordered.

READING

12

IN A DEMOCRACY, THE PEOPLE DECIDE

Susan M. Wolf

Susan M. Wolf is an associate professor of law and medicine at the University of Minnesota Law School and faculty member at the University's Center for Bioethics.

■ POINTS TO CONSIDER

1. Why does Wolf applaud the U.S. Supreme Court's decision?

2. Analyze the arguments in the New York and Washington State court challenges. Why did the U.S. Supreme Court unanimously reject them, according to the reading?

3. Summarize the various end-of-life issues the author mentions. In your opinion, what relationship do these have to the assisted suicide debate?

Wolf, Susan M. "Supreme Court Decision Rightly Forces More Talk About Life's End." **Star Tribune**. July 6, 1997: A17. Reprinted with permission from the **Star Tribune**, Minneapolis-St. Paul.

Our Constitution removes few debates from popular decision by assigning them to the courts. So it should be in a democracy.

The Supreme Court was right to send the question of whether to legalize physician-assisted suicide back to the states. Our Constitution removes few debates from popular decision by assigning them to the courts. So it should be in a democracy.

The Supreme Court justices applauded the thoughtful debate on assisted suicide already underway. California and Washington voters have rejected ballot initiatives to legalize the practice. The court noted that just recently Iowa and Rhode Island joined the great majority of states in prohibiting the practice. In Oregon, the sole state to legalize assisted suicide, the legislature has scheduled a reconsideration.

For the Supreme Court to invalidate state bans on assisted suicide would thus be anti-democratic. It would preempt a local decision on this very tough question. It would also, as the court said, "strike down the considered policy choice of almost every state."

STIFLING POPULAR CHOICE

Plaintiffs in Washington and New York had, in effect, asked the court to do exactly that. In the Washington case, plaintiffs argued that the 14th Amendment's liberty guarantee created a constitutional right to physician-assisted suicide. They pointed to the court's 1990 *Cruzan* decision suggesting a constitutional right to refuse life-sustaining treatment. If personal decisions such as treatment refusal were protected by the Constitution, why not assisted suicide?

Plaintiffs in the New York case brought their challenge from a different angle. They complained that New York allowed treatment refusal but forbade assisted suicide: This meant that only people "lucky enough" to be on life-sustaining treatment had a way to hasten death. But plaintiffs argued there was no rational distinction between terminating treatment and assisting suicide. They claimed that allowing one while banning the other violated the 14th Amendment's equal protection clause.

© **Tribune Media Services, Inc.**
Reprinted with permission.

EXAMINING ARGUMENTS

The Supreme Court unanimously rejected both arguments. The justices found it quite rational to distinguish treatment refusal from assisted suicide. The right to refuse is based on centuries of law protecting the right to reject unwanted bodily invasion. When doctors honor patients' right to refuse treatment, they let the underlying disease take its course. No medical system could operate ethically that routinely forced treatments on patients against their will.

Assisted suicide, however, is not rejection of invasive treatment. And a doctor who assists suicide is not letting disease take its course; rather the drugs (or other means offered) directly cause death. Anglo-American law has disapproved of assisted suicide for over 700 years. And permitting it raises deep concerns about error, abuse, and destroying patients' trust that physicians will honor their commitments to cure and care but never harm.

In reaching these conclusions the court did its job. But the court has not abandoned dying patients. Its *Cruzan* decision had already recognized a constitutional right to refuse life-sustaining treatment. That decision motivated Congress to enact the Patient

EVERYONE'S ISSUE

Although Laurence Tribe, in his own brief to the Court on assisted suicide, made a valiant effort to analogize those seeking physician assistance in dying to more traditional minorities, he is ultimately unpersuasive. All of us are going to die, whereas only a minority of us are, say, African-Americans or Jehovah's Witnesses.

Nor is the issue like that of abortion, where one can be confident that the males who dominate state legislatures never have to worry about being pregnant themselves. Every member of the legislature should be able to envision the possibility of being desperately ill and pleading with a doctor for prescriptions that will enable him or her to die....

Sanford Levison. "The Court's Death Blow." **The Nation.** July 21, 1997: 29.

Self-Determination Act, a law requiring health care institutions to honor living wills and other advance directives. And the court's decision strongly suggests a right to pain relief. They also acknowledge that doctors may give pain medication in the doses necessary to relieve pain, even if that risks respiratory depression and hastening death.

FOCUS ON THE END OF LIFE

This much is decided. We the people must shoulder the rest. We must make the rights declared work in the clinic. Too many people are never asked if they really want life-sustaining treatment. Even when patients write advance directives, they are often ignored. And too many people die with pain that could have been treated.

Hospice care must be widely available. Physicians need better training in terminal care. Health plans should have to report on their quality of care at the end of life. And the uninsured need health care to cope with terminal disease. Americans are right to fear dying, given this litany of deficiencies. Indeed, we have no idea what demand for assisted suicide would remain were we to solve even part of these problems.

We now face momentous work and debate. The Supreme Court has rightly entrusted us with both.

READING

13

THE COURTS FORSAKE
THE NEEDS OF REAL
PEOPLE

Jeffrey Kahn

Jeffrey Kahn is the director of the Center for Bioethics at the University of Minnesota and associate professor in the University's Medical School.

■ **POINTS TO CONSIDER**

1. Why is Kahn disappointed with the U.S. Supreme Court decision?

2. Discuss how this issue creates a conflict between the rights of the individual and the interests of the state.

3. Analyze the problem, as Kahn sees it, of some states allowing assisted suicide while others do not.

Kahn, Jeffrey. "Decision Merely Forces Those Who Want Right to Die to Go Out of State." **Star Tribune**. July 6, 1997: A17. Reprinted with permission of the **Star Tribune**, Minneapolis-St. Paul.

But we must do better by those to whom we owe respect for such an important and compelling interest than to beg off because of definitional shortsightedness or by resorting to warnings of the slippery slope.

Like most waiting for the Supreme Court decision on physician-assisted suicide last month, I wasn't surprised by the decision. But I am disappointed with the outcome.

The court decided that it could not endorse a constitutional right to assisted suicide and that states could properly enforce a ban on it as a matter of public policy. The court's decision forsakes the needs of real people for the sake of faceless policy, since it fails to address the needs of individual patients confronted with difficult choices as they face the end of life.

In his concurring opinion, Justice John Paul Stevens makes clear that the state's interest in a policy ban loses some of its compelling nature in individual cases and that similar reasoning that supports a court-recognized right to refuse life-sustaining treatment may apply to individuals requesting assisted suicide.

INDIVIDUALS OUTWEIGH STATE INTERESTS

He writes that the court's decision in the *Cruzan* case "makes it clear that some individuals who no longer have the option of deciding whether to live or to die because they are already on the threshold of death have a constitutionally protected interest in preserving life at all costs...It is an interest in deciding how, rather than whether, a critical threshold shall be crossed."

Policies admittedly need to be in place to serve and protect the interests of society and its citizens. Unfortunately, the court's decision abandons individuals' interests as they approach the "critical threshold" at the end of life in favor of focusing on serving social interests.

This decision tells individuals that their interest in a good death is not protected by our Constitution since the difficulty in determining what counts as "terminal illness" and in preventing abuse is too great.

JUSTICE FOR THOSE NEAR DEATH

But we must do better by those to whom we owe respect for

Life-support system

Cartoon by David Seavey. Copyright, **USA TODAY.**
Reprinted with permission.

such an important and compelling interest than to beg off because of definitional shortsightedness or by resorting to warnings of the slippery slope.

It is true, as critics of assisted suicide say, that there is a protected interest in refusal of life-sustaining treatment and that there is a *de facto* right to sufficient pain relief. Neither of these should be forsaken in a rush to embrace assisted suicide.

But in cases where there is no treatment to refuse and adequate pain relief cannot be achieved – and there will be such cases – individuals deserve to determine how they will cross the threshold between life and death.

A majority of Americans favor the individual right to assisted suicide – depending on the poll, anywhere from just over 50 percent to 70 percent. Because the court's decision has in effect shifted the debate to the states, now they will have a chance to exercise their voices.

Letting legislatures grapple with this issue allows states the opportunity to act as laboratories of the democratic process but adds its own complications. Some state will legalize assisted suicide in the not too distant future. Oregon has a ballot measure that could do just that, and it will experience an influx of willing patients.

TWO-TIERED SYSTEM

States will be categorized into those that will allow assisted suicide and those that will not, and patients will be forced to travel, to leave behind their loved ones, their physicians and all the rest of the people, places and things they should have around them as they cross the critical threshold.

Those too frail or sick to travel will be barred from exercising their rights, creating the ironic situation that those who most need to seek assistance are barred from it and creating a situation where a right is enjoyed or withheld by no more than a function of geography.

Any practice that would so intimately affect the lives of so many deserves to be debated in the most public forums possible. The court's decision to recognize each state's power to legislate this matter places the challenge squarely on the legislatures and those to whom they answer.

POLICIES V. PEOPLE

It is now time for the electorate to let its voice be heard. The Supreme Court passed the hard question to the states, and it is up to the states to confirm the court's view that such weighty issues are better left to the democratic process. Let's hope that we understand the difference between policies and people.

EXAMINING COUNTERPOINTS

This activity may be used as an individualized study guide for students in libraries and resource centers or as a discussion catalyst in small group and classroom discussions.

Point #1

The Supreme Court ruling is a disaster for individuals near death and in desperate pain. Dying patients are now at the mercy of state legislatures. These legislatures are less concerned with personal medical emergencies than they are with pleasing anti-assisted suicide special interest groups with power and money to sway the bodies that create law.

Counterpoint #1

The Supreme Court decision rightly leaves the decision of assisted suicide laws to the states. By not declaring a constitutional right-to-die, the decision whether or not to sanction physician-assisted suicide is left to the people through their state legislatures – not by decree of the court.

Point #2

The decision of the Supreme Court is a victory for advocates of decriminalization of physician-assisted suicice. To opponents' woe, it opens the door for continued debate on the issue – time for the growing contingent of supporters to mobilize advocacy campaigns in the states.

Counterpoint #2

The Supreme Court ruling is a threat to vulnerable people in the United States. Although not identifying a constitutional right-to-die, the Court appears sympathetic to the pro-euthanasia cause. The willingness expressed to hear further cases encourages doctors to defy the body of state laws already prohibiting the practice in order to challenge the laws.

Guidelines

Part A

Examine the counterpoints above and then consider the following questions:

1. Do you agree more with the Point or Counterpoint? Why?

2. Which readings in this book best illustrate Point #1 and Point #2?

3. Which readings best illustrate Counterpoint #1 and Counterpoint #2?

4. Do any cartoons in this book illustrate the meaning of any of the views expressed in the activity? Which ones and why?

Part B

Social issues are usually complex, but often problems become over-simplified in political debates and discussions. Usually a polarized version of social conflict does not adequately represent the diversity of views that surround social conflicts. Examine the counterpoints. Then write down possible interpretations of this issue other than the two arguments stated in the counterpoints.

CHAPTER 4

ENDANGERMENT OR EMPOWERMENT: THE ASSISTED SUICIDE DEBATE

DEATH WITH DIGNITY: THE POINT

Faye J. Girsh

Faye J. Girsh is the executive director of the Hemlock Society, U.S.A. Founded in 1980, the Hemlock Society advocates for public policy that decriminalizes physician-assisted suicide.

■ POINTS TO CONSIDER

1. List the precedents cited which, for Girsh, logically lead to legal physician-assisted suicide.

2. Discuss the meaning of "death with dignity" as the author presents it. What does the phrase "death with dignity" mean to you?

3. According to the reading, how could legal physician-assisted suicide relieve end-of-life anxieties? Do you agree with this? Why or why not?

Excerpted from Girsh, Faye. "The Case for Physician Aid in Dying." **Journal of the Hippocratic Society**. Fall 1997: 6-10. Reprinted with permission.

In a civilized society a person should be able to die quickly with dignity and certainty in the company of loved ones, if that is her wish.

The Hemlock Society was founded in 1980, shortly after the first "living will law" was passed in California in 1976; since then other organizations have developed. The mission of the Hemlock Society is to maximize the options for a dignified death, including voluntary physician aid in dying for terminally ill, mentally competent adults.

RIGHT-TO-DIE MOVEMENT

When the Hemlock Society was founded, "passive euthanasia" was just becoming acceptable, i.e., letting a patient die by refusal or removal of life support. It was a decade later that the Supreme Court, albeit weakly, affirmed the right of all Americans to refuse or withdraw unwanted medical treatment, including food and hydration, and to have an agent speak for them if they were incompetent. But that is not enough, since many patients who stop treatment die a prolonged and agonizing death and others do not have treatment to remove and so have no way to hasten their deaths.

Although there had been perfunctory legislation unsuccessfully introduced in the first half of this century, it was in 1988 that the recent attempts to pass laws permitting physician aid in dying began. In California the Humane and Dignified Death Act was proposed but did not get enough signatures to get on the ballot. In 1991, 46% of the voters in Washington supported Proposition 119. The following year a similar ballot measure, Proposition 161, was placed before the people of California and also received 46% of the vote. In 1994, 51% of the people of Oregon voted to permit physician aid in dying, using a prescribing-only model — the Oregon Death with Dignity law....

The issue is not one which affects just Americans. Since 1984 the Dutch have permitted physician-assisted suicide under strict judicial guidelines although no law has been passed. In Switzerland about 120 people on average have died each year with the help of physicians and members of the Exit Society following a law passed there 60 years ago allowing euthanasia if the intent is benign. The Northern Territory of Australia, under the Rights of the Terminally Ill Act, permitted four people with cancer to die with the help of a doctor from July 1996 to December 1996 before the law was repealed by the federal parliament. In 1997 in Colombia, a Catholic country, the Constitutional Court ruled that mercy killing should be decriminalized.

Why the growing consensus? Below I will list the reasons the Hemlock Society – and the majority of Americans polled – believe that providing physician-assisted dying for a terminally ill, mentally competent adult who requests it is a humane, compassionate, safe and effective option which should be made legal.

A DIGNIFIED DEATH

It is inhumane, cruel and even barbaric to make a suffering person, whose death is inevitable, live longer than he or she wishes. It is the final decision a person makes; there must be autonomy at that time of life if at no other. To quote legal philosopher Ronald Dworkin: "Making someone die in a way that others approve, but he believes is a horrifying contradiction of his life, is a devastating, odious form of tyranny."

It is necessary for physicians to be the agents of death if the person wants to die quickly, safely, peacefully and nonviolently since the best means to accomplish this is medication that only doctors can prescribe. There is no prohibition against a person killing oneself. In a civilized society a person should be able to die quickly with dignity and certainty in the company of loved ones, if that is her wish. Methods at the individual's disposal, however, are usually violent and uncertain, as well as traumatizing to the patient and the family....

With a terminally ill person, if physician-assisted dying were legal, the family could be present, good-byes could be said, and the death could be, as some family members who have openly participated describe it, a "wonderful" experience. And there would be no guilt that the person could have lived a full life had the hastened death not occurred since it would be at the patient's request, usually with the consultation of the family, and in the context of terminal illness....

FOR PROTECTION'S SAKE

Disabled, poor, elderly and minority people also want to die a good death. Polls of disabled individuals show a majority in support. A 1994 Harris poll found 66% of people with disabilities surveyed support a right to assisted dying. Between 63% and 90% of people with AIDS want this option and 55% have considered it for themselves.

Support is also strong from older Americans. A 1996 survey by *RxRemedy Magazine* of more than 30,000 people over 55 showed that 65% agreed that terminally people had a right to commit suicide with a doctor's assistance.

In the guise of protecting these groups, opponents argue that they would be hurt by an assisted dying law since they would be vulnerable. This "protection" not only deprives people who are not in these categories of choice and dignity in dying, it robs those very groups of this option with no evidence that this is a choice they would not want. In fact, evidence suggests that all people want this option, regardless of their status....

END-OF-LIFE ANXIETIES

People would live longer and better knowing there is help if the suffering becomes unbearable. The anxiety of not knowing how much longer one would have to suffer and watch the family suffer adds to the burden of terminal illness. Many people must end their lives prematurely through suicide while they are still able. Life could be extended if they knew help would be available from a physician.

Not all pain can be controlled. Even taking the best estimate from hospice, that 97% of pain is controllable, that still leaves 3% of dying people whose pain is unrelievable. What help is there for them? And, not all suffering is caused by physical pain. Surveys of patients in Holland who request aid in dying show that pain is fifth on the list of reasons why they ask for a hastened death. It is "senseless suffering" and the indignities of dependency, incontinence, and poor quality of life which lead them to request a hastened death. In addition, not all patients want the consequences of adequate pain control, which include diminution of cognitive function and severe constipation.

MORE THAN *DE FACTO* PRACTICE

Physician aid in dying is commonly practiced today in the United States. Doctors have always helped their patients end their suffering. If we are concerned about abuse of this practice, there should be controls and monitoring. In addition, it is a disservice to those people who cannot get help because they lack a personal relationship to their doctor, or who have a doctor who is unwilling to risk legal action and loss of license. No doctor has ever been convicted for helping a patient die, but those who do help often have to experience horrendous legal hassles before they are acquitted. Aid in dying must be regulated, legalized and above board so that doctors, families and patients can discuss it as part of the continuum of care. The process and criteria should be regulated and the outcomes reported. This is the way to prevent abuses and stop the slippery slope – not by driving it underground.

The issue will not go away. Increasingly, people are dying of chronic, debilitating illnesses such as cancer, neurological diseases, AIDS, and heart disease. This means longer periods of suffering and a prolongation of the dying process. People fear this extended dependency and want to know there is an end about which they can make a determination....

The abuses of not permitting lawful aid in dying far outweigh any that would arise if a carefully safeguarded law were in place. What we have now are botched attempts, trauma to the family, needless suffering on the part of patients and their loved ones, doctors who are helping without any type of oversight, and juries who acquit physicians and loved ones who help. Above all, there is an injustice to a dying individual who is denied the ultimate choice of deciding the time and manner of her death....

READING

15

DEATH WITH DIGNITY: THE COUNTERPOINT

Christopher Miles Coope

Christopher Miles Coope is senior research fellow in the School of Philosophy, University of Leads, England. Publications include "Abortion, Privacy and the Supreme: Is an Honorable Compromise Possible?" in Law, Computers and Artificial Intelligence, *1995, and "Does Teaching by Cases Mislead Us about Morality?" in* Journal of Medical Ethics, *1996.*

■ POINTS TO CONSIDER

1. Give one reason why Coope believes the phrase "death with dignity" is a tool of rhetoric rather than an argument of substance. Is dignity a subjective or objective term?

2. What notion, according to the reading, is important to discourage among patients?

3. In your estimation, why does the author want to bring attention away from the "kind of death" one has? What might be the problem with a society emphasizing able-bodiedness?

4. Discuss the author's rebuttal of the prominent philosophers' statement. With whom do you agree?

Coope, Christopher Miles. "Death with Dignity." **Hastings Center Report**. September/October 1997. Reprinted by permission, **Hastings Center Report**, Christopher Miles Coope.

It is thought somehow undignified to be ministered to as helpless. This is, I want to argue, an unreasonable and mischievous thought...But I fear that talk of "death with dignity" will create a climate in which such things are thought undignified...

Those who argue in favor of euthanasia will characteristically want to relieve suffering. Perhaps too, where the patient appears to be in a persistent vegetative state, there will be a wish to see medical resources being put to a better use. But there is thought to be a third advantage: people, it is said, should be able to die with dignity. Euthanasia, it would be suggested, is not merely a matter of mercy killing, or resource saving. It is sometimes a matter of respect. No doubt people will say the same thing about its twin, assisted suicide....

What then would be meant by this wish that someone should die with dignity? What would be its content? It is not quite obvious what is at issue. The phrase "death with dignity" might just have found its way into circulation without having much sense behind it. And why, one wonders, is it used so selectively?...

SUBJECTIVE APPROACH

It is sometimes suggested that we might take a subjective approach to this question, saying that if someone merely thinks that a certain way of dying is undignified then it would be undignified for this individual to die in this way. It is easy to see why this idea is popular, for it seems to bypass our problems with definition, and it has an attractive air of autonomy about it. But it is plainly no solution to our current worries. For if no one understands the phrase "death without dignity" we likewise do not understand the sentence, "Smith thinks that this is a death without dignity." And if we did understand "death without dignity" we should not in any case be saying that a dying person who merely thinks he is dying without dignity must thereby be dying in such a manner. Dignity is related to insult. Being insulted is something quite objective: a sensitive person can think he is being insulted when this is quite untrue. This latter point is in fact quite important, for in the current climate more and more people will come to have these thoughts or quasi thoughts and perhaps need to be helped to think better....

"RESPECTFUL-IN-ITSELF"

One can of course die in rather undignified circumstances. One would not want to be caught with one's trousers down in a brothel. But circumstances apart, can the sort of death that just happens naturally be dignified or undignified? Smith dies while twitching; Robinson does not twitch. One is perhaps inclined to say that Smith's death is the more dignified. Why? Partly perhaps because some deaths are particularly distressing to bystanders. But as this seems hardly relevant, we look for something else....

We can thus give this notion a tenuous sense. But ought we? I think we should not fuss. It is bad enough dealing with bereavement, without having the additional worry, which culturally could get out of hand, whether the death was not only instantaneous or pain-free but somehow respectful-in-itself. Someone whose friend or spouse or child is killed in a road accident would, amid their other troubles, find themselves worrying whether this was a sufficiently solemn way to go.

ANXIETY ABOUT HELPLESSNESS

And there is a further disadvantage. People who talk about death with dignity are often not thinking of death, but of the state that precedes it. The individual in question may not be dying at all. Tony Bland was not dying as he lay in that bed – his not dying, in the view of some, was just the trouble. It is thought somehow undignified to be ministered to as helpless. This is, I want to argue, an unreasonable and mischievous thought, and it is especially important for doctors, nurses, and caregivers to discourage it. Just as we all once needed our nappies changed, a process without the least trace of insult, so those of us who are temporarily able-bodied may one day need this service again. Any service can be provided in a way that shows lack of respect. But neither being in need, nor being helped, should be thought demeaning in itself. Why should it? But I fear that talk of "death with dignity" will create a climate in which such things are thought undignified, and someone who then simply laughs and says, "Poppycock!" will be deemed insensitive. Of course, a caregiver will need to be sensitive to people's concerns, even if these concerns are unreasonable. But the encouragement of this kind of concern is a harm to all those who need this kind of help.

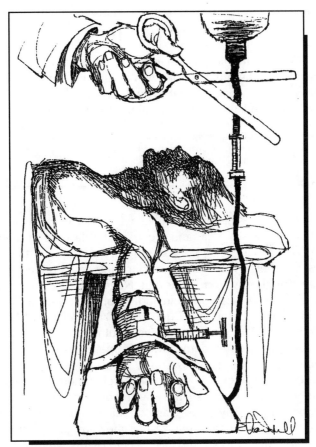

Illustration by Eleanor Mill.
Reprinted with permission.

SENSITIVITIES

It might be thought – and this is a point about euthanasia – that one would be insulted by a doctor who refused to kill one on request. But that would surely depend upon the doctor's reason. He might be too busy with another patient. He might think that it is wrong to kill – so that he would not do the deed himself or hand the patient over for it to be done by another. Both reasons are quite compatible with respect. And if one died the next day of natural causes would it follow that this death was somehow undignified, being not what one asked for? What would such a claim mean?

"Most of us see death – whatever we think will follow it – as the
final act of life's drama, and we want that last act to reflect our
own convictions, those we have tried to live by, not the convictions of others forced on us in our most vulnerable moment,"
wrote Ronald Dworkin, Thomas Nagel, Robert Nozick, John
Rawls, Thomas Scanlon, and Judith Jarvis Thomson ("Assisted
Suicide: The Philosophers' Brief," *New York Review of Books*, 27
March 1997). This might sound well, but in truth it is a somewhat
confused passage to come from the pen of so many eminent
philosophers. There is no reason to suppose that those who think
that abetting a suicide is wrong are forcing their conviction on a
patient merely because they will not allow his wish to be
"helped" in this way to be granted. This kind of sloppy talk is so
usual that people hardly realize that they are going in for it. It is
meant, of course, to suggest disrespect. That is why we have this
hint of brainwashing, though it is quite inappropriate.

LIFE LEGACY?

There is also a story in circulation — it seems for example to
have caught the ear of Justice Stevens, to go by his recent remarks
in *Washington v. Glucksberg* — that one is likely, in the main, to
be remembered by one's friends in the condition of one's last
infirmity. If one had dribbled one would forevermore be a drib-
bler. One would have been remembered with honor, by contrast,
if one had perished suddenly in one's undribbling prime. But who
is there who has such peculiar friends? If one is unfortunate
enough to be burdened with them, it is surely this habit of linking
indignity with incapacity which has made them that way.

Ronald Dworkin, in his book *Life's Dominion* (London: Harper Collins, 1993, p. 212), quotes Nietzsche's *The Twilight of the Idols* approvingly: "In a certain state it is indecent to live longer. To go on vegetating in cowardly dependence on physicians and machinations...ought to prompt a profound contempt in society." Nietzsche also said that one should "die proudly when it was no longer possible to live proudly." But these thoughts are romantic, and romanticism in life, though not always perhaps in art, is an invitation to folly and disaster: it is the substitution of what appears impressive for what is true. How could Tony Bland sensibly be supposed to have suffered from cowardice while comatose? How could it have been indecent merely to be alive?

SHRINKING OUR VOCABULARY

All in all, we have seen too much "profound contempt" for the weak and the injured in the century since Nietzsche wrote these fancy words. For these various reasons then, I suggest that the phrase "death with dignity," never very clear in the first place, should be given up.

READING

16

HOSPICE, NOT HEMLOCK

Joe Loconte

Joe Loconte is the deputy editor of Policy Review, *a conservative journal of politics and culture. He is also the author of* Seducing the Samaritan: How Government Contracts Are Reshaping Social Services *(Pioneer Institute for Public Policy Research).*

■ POINTS TO CONSIDER

1. The article discusses two polar options concerning the manner in which people die. Describe these and explain the author's point of view on this dichotomy.

2. Explain "hospice" and "palliative care" as understood in the reading.

3. How has the hospice movement contributed to pain management?

4. Why is pain management integral to hospice care?

Excerpted from Loconte, Joe. "Hospice, Not Hemlock: The Medical and Moral Rebuke of Doctor-Assisted Suicide." **Policy Review**. March/April 1998: 40-48. Reprinted with permission of **Policy Review**.

Hospice programs are, in fact, the only institution in the country with a record of compassionate, end-of-life care for people with incurable illnesses. The hospice movement, and the palliative approach to medicine it represents, could revolutionalize America's culture of dying.

In the deepening debate over assisted suicide, almost everyone agrees on a few troubling facts: Most people with terminal illnesses die in the sterile settings of hospitals or nursing homes, often in prolonged, uncontrolled pain; physicians typically fail to manage their patients' symptoms, adding mightily to their suffering; the wishes of patients are ignored as they are subjected to intrusive, often futile, medical interventions; and aggressive end-of-life care often bankrupts families that are already in crisis.

Too many people in America are dying a bad death.

HOSPICE OR HEMLOCK?

The solution, some tell us, is physician-assisted suicide. Oregon has legalized the practice for the terminally ill. Michigan's Jack Kevorkian continues to help willing patients end their own lives. The prestigious *New England Journal of Medicine* has come out in favor of doctor-assisted death. Says Faye Girsh, the director of the Hemlock Society: "The only way to achieve a quick and painless and certain death is through medications that only a physician has access to."

This, we are told, is death with dignity. What we do not often hear is that there is another way to die – under the care of a specialized discipline of medicine that manages the pain of deadly diseases, keeps patients comfortable yet awake and alert, and surrounds the dying with emotional and spiritual support. Every year, roughly 450,000 people die in this way. They die in hospice....

The hospice concept rejects decisions to hasten death, but also extreme medical efforts to prolong life for the terminally ill. Rather, it aggressively treats the symptoms of disease – pain, fatigue, disorientation, depression – to ease the emotional suffering of those near death. It applies "palliative medicine," a team-based philosophy of caregiving that unites the medical know-how of doctors and nurses with the practical and emotional support of social workers, volunteer aids, and spiritual counselors. Because the goal of hospice is comfort, not cure, patients are usually treated at home, where most say they would prefer to die.

"Most people nowadays see two options: A mechanized, depersonalized, and painful death in a hospital or a swift death that rejects medical institutions and technology," says Nicholas Christakis, an assistant professor of medicine and sociology at the University of Chicago. "It is a false choice. Hospice offers a way out of this dilemma."

A NEW VISION OF MEDICINE

Hospice programs are, in fact, the only institution in the country with a record of compassionate, end-of-life care for people with incurable illnesses. The hospice movement, and the palliative approach to medicine it represents, could revolutionize America's culture of dying.

Since the mid-1970s, hospice programs have grown from a mere handful to more than 2,500, available in nearly every community. At least 4,000 nurses are now nationally certified in hospice techniques. In Michigan – Kevorkian's home state – a statewide hospice program cares for 1,100 people a day, regardless of their ability to pay. The Robert Wood Johnson Foundation, a leading health care philanthropy, has launched a $12-million initiative to improve care for the dying. And the American Medical Association, which did not even recognize hospice as a medical discipline until 1995, has made the training of physicians in end-of-life care one of its top priorities.

There is a conflict raging in America today over society's obligations to care for its most vulnerable. Says Charles von Gunten, a hospice specialist at Northwestern Memorial Hospital, in Chicago, "It is fundamentally an argument about the soul of medicine." One observer calls it a choice between hospice or hemlock – between a compassion that "suffers with" the dying, or one that eliminates suffering by eliminating the sufferer.

A MOVEMENT TAKING HOLD

The modern hospice movement was founded by English physician Cicely Saunders, who, as a nurse in a London clinic, was aghast at the disregard for the emotional and spiritual suffering of patients near death. In 1967, she opened St. Christopher's Hospice, an in-patient facility drawing on spiritual and practical

112

support from local congregations....

Early hospice programs were independent and community-run, managed by local physicians or registered nurses. Most operated on a shoestring, relying on contributions, patient payments, and private insurance. Many were relatively spartan, consisting of little more than a nurse and a social worker making home visits.

Religious communities were early and natural supporters....

By the mid-1980s, the movement started to take off. As hospital costs escalated, Medicare joined a growing number of insurance companies that offered reimbursement for hospice's home-care approach. In 1985, President Ronald Reagan signed legislation making the Medicare hospice benefit a permanent part of the Medicare program.

Today nearly 80 percent of hospices qualify. Medicare picks up most of the bill for services, from pain medications to special beds. The majority of managed-care plans offer at least partial coverage, and most private insurance plans include a hospice benefit. Since becoming a part of Medicare, hospice has seen a four-fold increase in patients receiving its services....

LOSING CONTROL

Hardly anything creates a more frightening sense of chaos than unrelieved pain and suffering. "We know that severe pain greatly reduces people's ability to function," says Patricia Berry, the director of the Wisconsin Cancer Pain Initiative. "If we don't control symptoms, then people can't have quality of life, they can't choose what they want to do or what to think about."

By interrupting sleep, curbing appetite, and discouraging personal interactions, pain doesn't just aggravate a person's physical condition. It also leads, as a recent report by the Institute of Medicine puts it, to "depression and demoralization" of the sufferer. Says David English, the president of the Hospice of Northern Virginia, one of the nation's oldest programs, "You can't address the psychosocial issues of a person who is in pain."

Hospice has understood this connection between pain and overall well-being from the start. After conventional treatments fail, says Martha Twaddle, "you'll often hear doctors say 'there's nothing left to do.' There's a lot left to do. There is a lot of aggressive care that can be given to you to treat your symptoms."

Hardly anyone doubts that more energetic caregiving for the dying is in order. A 1990 report from the National Cancer Institute warned that "undertreatment of pain and other symptoms of cancer is a serious and neglected public health problem." The New York State Task Force on Life and the Law, in arguing against legalizing assisted suicide, cited the "pervasive failure of our health-care system to treat pain and diagnose and treat depression...."

PAIN MANAGEMENT AND COMFORT

The pain control approach of hospice depends on an aggressive use of opioid drugs – narcotics such as morphine, fentanyl, codeine, or methadone....

Physicians and other authorities outside the hospice movement agree that most pain can be controlled. Authors of the New York Task Force report assert that "modern pain relief techniques can alleviate pain in all but extremely rare cases." A primer on cancer pain management from the U.S. Department of Health and Human Services (HHS) urges clinicians to "reassure patients and families that most pain can be relieved safely and effectively."

The wide acceptance of the use of morphine and other narcotics to control pain owes much to hospice caregivers. The key people at a World Health Organization conference, which helped establish the HHS guidelines on pain control, were leaders in hospice care. Says James Cleary, the director of palliative medicine at the University of Wisconsin Medical School: "The whole concept of providing good palliative care has really been driving the movement...."

Research studies from at least 1980 onward demonstrate that opioid use does not lead to addiction among acute pain sufferers. Physical dependence – not the same as addiction – becomes a problem when medication is quickly discontinued, but experts say it can be easily managed by gradually reducing dosages. Psychological addiction, even when high doses of narcotics are given, does not seem to occur.

The most widely cited studies on drug addiction show that morphine only becomes psychologically addictive in people with a history of substance abuse, or when it is used for reasons other than managing serious pain. "I've been with hospice for over 20 years," Berry says, "and I've never seen anybody become psychologically dependent." In a review of 10,000 burn patients requir-

114

ing large amounts of opioid therapy, none were reported to have become addicted. The M.D. Anderson Cancer Center in Houston, citing the best clinical studies, discounts the risk of opioid addiction when used to treat pain....

SAVING THE SOUL OF MEDICINE

Even the goal of easing people's suffering, as central as it is to hospice care, is not an end in itself. The aim of comfort is part of a larger objective: to help the terminally ill live as fully as possible until they die. This is where hospice departs most pointedly both from traditional medicine and the advocates of assisted suicide....

Hospice or hemlock: Though both end in death, each pursues its vision of a "good death" along radically different paths. At its deepest level, the hospice philosophy strikes a blow at the notion of the isolated individual. It insists that no one dies in a vacuum. Where one exists, hospice physicians, nurses, and social workers rush in to help fill it....

We seem, as a culture, to be under such a test, and the outcome is not at all certain. Some call it a war for the soul of medicine. If so, hospice personnel could be to medical care what American GIs were to the Allied effort in Europe – the source of both its tactical and moral strength and, eventually, the foot soldiers for victory and reconstruction.

HOSPICE CARE OR ASSISTED SUICIDE: A FALSE DICHOTOMY

John L. Miller, M.A.

John L. Miller, M.A. is the executive director of the Trinity Home Hospice in Toronto, Ontario.

■ POINTS TO CONSIDER

1. Consult the readings in Chapter One. Compare and contrast Miller's suggested guidelines for assisted suicide to those which govern euthanasia and assisted suicide in the Netherlands.

2. Explain the "false dichotomy" in the article.

3. Summarize Miller's view concerning the "slippery slope" argument.

4. Why does the author support legal rights to physician-assisted suicide?

Excerpted from Miller, John L. "Hospice Care or Assisted Suicide: A False Dichotomy." **The American Journal of Hospice and Palliative Care**. May/June 1997: 132, 134. Reprinted with permission, **The American Journal of Hospice and Palliative Care**.

Reforms must happen in a context where we continue to promote alternatives, where we understand that several things can be true at the same time: Hospice care is wonderful for some. Physician-assisted suicide is a valid choice for others.

The view expressed here is one which comes from within the hospice movement, but which supports legal reforms to allow physician-assisted suicide.

Specifically, the legal reforms I am referring to would require many important safeguards which Dr. Kevorkian does not implement. A responsible assisted suicide would require free and repeated requests by the patient, with a substantial interval between requests. The involvement of a third party in a suicide ethically requires us to make sure the suffering is not temporary, or due to lack of information or obtainable (and desired) treatment. Informed consent, confirmed by two independent medical practitioners, would be required only after all available alternatives have been offered and explored. The fine details of these conditions are, of course, much debated. This article, however, looks not at these details, but at the ethical justification for such a position.

To begin, I applaud the promotion of hospice care in the media. Promoting compassionate palliative care to the general public is essential, especially if one believes that physician-assisted suicide should be made available in the context of offering choices.

NOT ONE MORAL CHOICE

But the "Dr. Dignity" program does not promote hospice care as just a choice. It promotes it as the only moral choice, and, in doing so, sets up a false dichotomy....One might mistakenly conclude that all proponents of legal reform were either historically naive, ignorant of hospice and palliative care, or both. And while some people may be guilty of this lack of information, many others are not.

Many people who have devoted their lives to the care of the dying are not opposed to physician-assisted suicide. Such people believe it should be available as one of several options, and, therefore, do not believe that promoting hospice, and advocating for the availability of regulated physician-assisted suicide are contradictory goals.

CLARIFYING THE DEBATE

Understanding this position begins with an understanding of how and why assisted suicide and euthanasia differ. Not surprisingly, most people in the general public do not know the difference between the two terms; opponents of assisted suicide often deliberately obscure these differences by using the terms interchangeably.

But, many people support legalized assisted suicide for the same reason that they oppose euthanasia: the first offers us life choices and power over our own bodies, while the second takes control and choices away from us. Hospice care also offers people an essential choice, and so, on we campaign to make it available, and to make it better.

⚬ The problem with hospice care, however, is that in spite of our best public relations efforts, it doesn't always take away people's pain, and it isn't always wanted.

Parallels are often drawn between this debate, and the one on abortion rights. These parallels are indeed apt. And since the war of words is as confusing there as it is here, let's blow away the fog: Mainstream proponents of legalized assisted suicide advocate for its availability not because they are pro-death, but because they believe in a person's right to control his/her life, and the right of a person to a death which s/he feels is dignified (even if we don't agree that it is).

In the assisted suicide debate, opponents sometimes use logical fallacies and historical misinformation to point fear at the wrong menace. It is easy to quell dissent in this way.

SLIPPERY SLOPE

Take the argument, for instance, that assisted suicide will lead to euthanasia, eugenics, or even genocide. For a "slippery slope" argument to be valid, there must be a connection between an initial minor, social ill, and a potentially more serious one – an ill which, when amplified incrementally, creeps up on us and finally, has catastrophic, societal results. This connection usually exists because the minor social ill is of the same kind as the more serious one, and because taking one step makes the next one easier.

In this case, it is not valid to link assisted suicide to the more

118

serious threat of euthanasia, eugenics, and genocide simply because they all involve third parties in the death of another person. One of these things is not like the others. To link them in this way is as ridiculous as saying that electing a government to make state decisions leads to a fascism. Just because both involve state rule doesn't mean that giving a government power inevitably leads to its absolute power. A slippery slope to fascism happens when the checks which make governments representative and accountable are subtly removed, one by one.

Fear of a societal erosion of personal autonomy is a valid concern. The response must be to give people more choices, not fewer; more autonomy, not less. The legal reforms I offer for debate move us further away from fascism, not towards it.

If assisted suicide were an act, which in some small way diminished a person's power of self-determination, then one might make an argument that allowing such an act pushes us down a slippery slope toward more serious violations of this kind. The slow whittling away of self-determination can creep up on us, if we don't watch out.

EXPANDING HUMAN CHOICE

And so, concerns should be expressed when laws which erode people's rights are created, or when existing rights legislation is revoked. Concern should be expressed when states give power to medical practitioners to override informed consent.

In remembering history, let's remember that this is exactly what occurred in Nazi-occupied Europe. Under the Nazis, "physician-assisted suicide" was never any such thing. It was always murder, the taking of someone's life against his/her will. Doctors assisted in these murders in a context where Jews and other minorities had no rights of any kind, and where neither quality of life, nor life itself were valued.

It is indeed conceivable that personal freedoms may be eroded in North America. But the top of the slippery slope is not assisted-suicide. If anything, the "slope" is the loss of personal autonomy, and it exists already. We're teetering on the edge, and proponents of assisted suicide are reaching out to help pull us back up, not to push us down.

A FOREIGN PERSPECTIVE

Because I am writing in Avignon in Provence, the deep South of France, I am struck by the silence that greets the topic of physician-assisted suicide in the French media, which on other issues seem almost obsessed with America....Where it is addressed, foreign observers see it in a polemically cultural guise, as yet another indication that American culture – stereotyped as overly optimistic, superficial, youth-oriented – is unable to assimilate the complexities and darker, more morally ambiguous aspects of human experience.

Arthur Kleinman. "Intimations of Solidarity?" **Hastings Center Report.** September/October 1997: 36.

If, in North America, the right to control our bodies and our lives is further eroded in any significant way, physician-assisted suicide would certainly never become available. Women's reproductive rights would also be targets (they already are), as would informed consent in any medical decision, including one involving hospice care.

OTHER MORAL ALTERNATIVES

Dressing up hospice care as a panacea, and the only moral alternative to physician-assisted suicide is unhelpful, and inaccurate.

This issue is not simplistic. Reforms must happen in a context where we continue to promote alternatives, where we understand that several things can be true at the same time: Hospice care is wonderful for some. Physician-assisted suicide is a valid choice for others. People will always seek to influence the vulnerable and the sick. With freedoms come responsibilities.

Disabled rights activists, and indeed those of us in the hospice movement, know that it is not just the state which can coerce people to make unwanted or unnecessary choices. Family members, friends, peers, can also put subtle pressures on loved ones to choose a path which is better for the well person than for the sick.

But these pressures work both ways, unfortunately. Just as there are those who pressure people they love to end it all, there are also those who push people unduly to "hang on until the end." Knowing when to step back, knowing when to move forward, finding this balance in supporting the dignity of those we care for – this is the previous challenge with which we are all entrusted in hospice care.

CONSTANT VIGILANCE

We must be wary of the danger of falling to the extremes. At one end are those who value life at all cost – even at the expense of quality. At this end, preventing another person from ending his/her life regardless of the circumstances is seen as acceptable. At the other end are those who put quality of life first, but who also believe that they can know how good or bad someone else's life is. People who think this way can be equally dangerous, because they feel no qualms about either pressuring us to end our life if they feel we are too miserable, or pressuring us to hang on, if they decide for us that our life is still worth living.

When we fall to the extremes, we take choices away from those who we believe we are helping. But, there is a middle ground. When we aim for that middle ground, we all win.

READING

18

ASSISTED SUICIDE AND MANAGED CARE: A DANGER TO THE PUBLIC

Daniel Sulmasy, M.D., Ph.D.

Daniel Sulmasy, M.D., Ph.D., is an assistant professor in the Division of General Internal Medicine and director of the Center for Bioethics at Georgetown University. He also holds a doctorate in philosophical ethics.

■ POINTS TO CONSIDER

1. Describe the two movements in health care which the author highlights.

2. Discuss health care costs in the United States. What regimes have been implemented for health care cost containment?

3. Evaluate the author's contention of the dangers of legal assisted suicide in an era of managed care.

4. According to the author, how will physician-assisted suicide affect the doctor/patient relationship?

5. Why does the physician-assisted suicide proponents' "privacy argument" fail for Sulmasy?

Excerpted from Sulmasy, Daniel. "Managed Care and Managed Death." **Archives of Internal Medicine**, vol. 155. January 23, 1995: 133-6. Copyright 1995, American Medical Association. Reprinted with permission.

If euthanasia and assisted suicide are legalized in a system of managed competition, conflicts will also inevitably arise in managing the deaths of those who cannot speak for themselves.

Currently, more than 13% of the American gross national product is derived from health care. It is widely believed that this amount of health care expenditure is excessive and must be controlled.

There are many proposals to try to fix the health care system. For a variety of reasons, not convincing to all, it now seems that some form of "managed competition" will play an important role in government efforts to control health care costs.

HEALTH CARE AND COST CONTAINMENT

Under managed competition, both not-for-profit and for-profit health insurance companies and large health care systems would be asked to compete with each other within limits set by governmental agencies in an attempt to control health care costs through market forces. The key to the economic success of many of these large health care systems, like Health Maintenance Organizations (HMOs), is the concept of "managed care." In managed care, each patient is assigned a primary care physician who acts as a "gatekeeper," keeping patients from consuming health care dollars by limiting the use of expensive tests, treatments, and specialty care. Gatekeepers are usually given financial incentives to control costs while maintaining quality. What is envisioned under managed competition is thus a three-layered system. The government manages HMOs, HMOs manage physicians, and physicians manage patients. All three would have strong incentives to spend less on health care....

MANAGED DEATH

A growing number of Americans have begun to call for the legalization of euthanasia and assisted suicide. The reasons for this are varied and complex. Some Americans probably have a deep sense of having lost control over their lives in the face of an ever increasing use of medical technology, and seem to feel that by dying when, where, and how they choose, they can assert some measure of personal control over and against this technology. Doubtless others are afraid — afraid of death itself, afraid of

123

pain, afraid of dying alone and forgotten. Some are driven by a distinctively American sense of pragmatism and individualism. Still others are implicitly utilitarian, believing that regardless of the means, the right decision is the one that results in the most net happiness for everyone involved....

As the campaign continues, new terminology has emerged. Some advocates of euthanasia and assisted suicide have recently adopted the phrase "managed death" to suggest the ease and professionalism with which euthanasia and assisted suicide might be accomplished....

THE LOGIC OF BEING A BURDEN

As providers of managed care, many physicians will be motivated by concern for quality, but concerns about cost will also be significant. Their concern for quality will probably be made explicit, but their concern for cost will generally be left unspoken. As providers of managed death, many physicians will be sincerely motivated by respect for patient autonomy, but the cost factor will always lurk silently in the background. This will be especially true if they are providing managed death in a setting of managed care. A perilous line of argument might then emerge from between the lines of the physician's soliloquy: (1) Too much money is being spent on health care; (2) Certain patients are expensive to take care of (i.e., those with physical and mental disabilities and the elderly); (3) These patients appear to suffer a great deal, lead lives of diminished dignity, and are a burden to others, both emotionally and financially; (4) Recognizing the diminished dignity, suffering, and burdens borne by these persons and those around them, their right to euthanasia or assisted suicide should be legally recognized; and (5) The happy side effect will be health care cost savings....

The emotional weight of this logic will press heavily on encounters between physicians and patients under managed care. The conflict of interest created by trying to make the physician both the agent of care and the agent of cost containment will come to a climax once HMOs begin to provide euthanasia and assisted suicide. The drama will be heightened by the soft tones and the ambiguous motives of the physician....

More cynical patients might see a thinly veiled conflict of interest. The facts would be such that physicians would make

more money if their patients were to die. Patients might come to fear their physicians. The already tarnished notion of trust in one's physician might suffer even more decay.

MANAGING THE VOICELESS

If euthanasia and assisted suicide are legalized in a system of managed competition, conflicts will also inevitably arise in managing the deaths of those who cannot speak for themselves. No one will argue that vulnerable members of our society should be involuntarily killed (i.e., against their wishes). But it has been argued convincingly that nonvoluntary euthanasia (i.e., without a specific request by the patient because the patient is incompetent) would quickly follow the legalization of voluntary euthanasia or assisted suicide in the United States. If these activities were initially legalized only for those capable of making voluntary choices, American constitutional law, under the due process and equal protection principles, would almost automatically extend the right to euthanasia and assisted suicide to those who are incapable of expressing choices, such as the retarded, the mentally disturbed, and the demented. In fact, such nonvoluntary euthanasia has now become common in the Netherlands. Thus, managed care systems would have an incentive to ask relatives of such vulnerable persons to agree to euthanasia for their loved ones. Euthanasia for such patients would be in the best financial interest of all levels of management – the government, the HMO, and the physician.

REAL DANGERS

Some might feel that the concerns expressed herein are exaggerated. But this would not seem to be the case. First, the scenario seems subtle. In fact, some might not see that this text demonstrates anything morally troubling. I would argue that if anyone is so convinced of the necessity of cost control that he or she cannot see a conflict of interest in this scenario, then he or she is symptomatic of the problem itself, and not a credible voice raised in argument against it. Second, these mixed motives are already becoming explicit. Studies have already been conducted to examine whether advance directives save money. Physicians have argued that those who have advance directives ought to receive an incentive discount on their health insurance because this could save the health care system millions of dollars....

Finally, one should note that there is evidence that financial incentives for physicians in HMOs are effective. Subtle changes toward more cost-effective behavior actually happen with the right incentives. Managed death would be a chillingly effective way to control the cost of managed care.

THE ARGUMENT FAILS

Others might grant that the dangers of such abuse are real, but would argue that effective safeguards can be instituted. Yet this argument raises more problems than it solves. First, one must recognize the paradox in this argument. On the one hand, euthanasia is justified on the grounds of privacy. But on the other hand, recognizing the potential for abuse, it is argued that euthanasia should be anything but a private event, open to careful scrutiny, so that all the abuses can be detected and prosecuted. It is never a good idea to correct a plan by introducing solutions that contradict its justification. Second, even if one were to open this sort of practice to public scrutiny, the sort of abuse suggested by the scenario is subtle and would be difficult to measure. Third, no matter what new peer review process or additional bureaucratic mechanism one were to develop, the conflict of interest would remain. A conflict of interest arises solely because of the structure

126

ELDERLY AT RISK

Individuals under age twenty-five make up 16% of the U.S. population and account for 16% of all suicides; those 65 and older make up 12% of the population and account for 21% of all suicides (NCHS, 1990). Older adults are also the most likely to be dying.

Excerpted from the testimony of Nancy J. Osgood before the Subcommittee on Health and Environment of the U.S. House of Representatives Commerce Committee, March 6, 1997.

of a relationship. It does not depend on the words and actions of the conflicted party. Finally, the fact that it has proven so difficult to stop Kevorkian from assisting with suicides under current strict laws should warn us that a more liberal law with provisions for careful scrutiny will be unlikely to effectively prevent abuse....

MORALLY PROBLEMATIC COMBINATION

Some do not believe that assisted suicide and euthanasia are, in themselves, morally problematic activities for the medical profession. Yet even persons so persuaded will at least recognize that legalizing euthanasia and assisted suicide at a time of intense pressure to control the cost of health care is unwise. Like alcohol and gasoline, managed care and managed death do not mix.

READING

19

COST CUTTING MUST EXIT OUR DISCOURSE

David B. McCurdy

David B. McCurdy is co-director of clinical health care ethics support services at Park Ridge Center for the Study of Health, Faith and Ethics in Chicago. His article appeared in The Christian Century, *a weekly ecumenical journal of discourse on current events and culture.*

■ POINTS TO CONSIDER

1. Describe the shift in definition that has occurred, according to McCurdy.

2. Why does the author caution euthanasia opponents about associating euthanasia with Nazi Genocide?

3. What is the meaning of euthanasia's Greek root? Evaluate the significance of this meaning to McCurdy's article.

McCurdy, David B. "Saying What We Mean." **The Christian Century**. 17-24 July 1996: 708-9. Copyright 1996 Christian Century Foundation. Reprinted by permission from the July 17-24, 1996, issue of **The Christian Century**.

Those who would deny life-sustaining treatments in order to conserve resources should not be allowed, let alone encouraged, to call the consequences of their proposal "euthanasia."

A subtle shift in habits of thought and language has infiltrated discussions of euthanasia and related issues. The prevalent understanding of euthanasia as an action or an omission of treatment motivated by mercy has been joined to – and sometimes replaced by – a conception of euthanasia as an economically motivated denial of medical treatment.

Not surprisingly, this shift occurs at a time when economic considerations are playing an increasing role in public policy discussions of the morality and legality of euthanasia. Economic arguments have long been employed both to support and to oppose public sanction of euthanasia. What has changed is that, in some instances, economic considerations have become part of the definition of euthanasia.

A clear example of this shift occurs in a *New York Times* op-ed piece addressing the congressional debate over Medicare reform. Burke J. Balch, a representative of the National Right to Life Committee, worries that private managed care plans will lead to the rationing of life-sustaining medical treatments. In opposing such rationing, he claims that "denial of life-saving medical treatment against the patient's will amounts to involuntary euthanasia."

MERCY, NOT MONEY

His fears should be taken seriously. The argument that supports his view, however, relies on an unacknowledged replacement of the generally accepted meaning of euthanasia with an understanding of euthanasia as the product of a cost-benefit assessment.

Those who debated the morality of euthanasia in the 1970s and 1980s generally agreed that euthanasia was characterized by a merciful desire to relieve another's suffering or end mere existence in a hopeless condition. A deliberate action or an omission of treatment that led to a person's death was termed euthanasia only if its intent was beneficient – if it sought the patient's good – and was motivated by compassion. This understanding is still widely shared, even among opponents of euthanasia.

In the National Right to Life Committee's grim depiction of managed Medicare, however, the real force behind "euthanasia" is the overriding drive to save money. Beneficence is barely in view, and compassion is nowhere to be seen.

RESHAPING THE ARGUMENT

If this definitional shift appeared only in one special interest group's polemic, it might merit little attention, but similar deviations have also appeared in the writings of philosophers and bioethicists – those who might be expected to act as guardians of moral discourse.

Some of these authors seem unaware of the shift they make. Philosopher Larry Churchill observes that opponents of a proposal to ration medical treatment on the basis of age are wrong to characterize the proposal as "advocating passive euthanasia for the elderly on utilitarian grounds." Yet Churchill overlooks the most crucial point. Such opponents of age-rationing not only allege that "passive euthanasia" has a utilitarian justification; they also redefine "passive euthanasia" as an economically based denial of treatment. They then feel free to charge that "euthanasia" is the intent of the proposed rationing of care. By failing to note the redefinition, Churchill is drawn into the new use and appears to concede its legitimacy.

GOOD DEATH CONSERVES RESOURCES

Other writers are more deliberate about shifting the definition. Bioethicist Margaret Pabst Battin observes that society is "coming to use the term euthanasia not just for pain-sparing deaths but for resource-conserving deaths as well." She comments that euthanasia's Greek root meaning "good death," a death that is good for the patient, is thereby compromised, and she decries the change: "Our very language invites us to overlook distinctions that we ought to make." Yet after noting society's rapid change in usage, Battin adopts the economically based definition herself. She argues that justice requires "the practice of euthanasia" as resource-saving denial of treatment "in certain kinds of scarcity situations."

Right-to-life activists alter their usage for different purposes. The National Right to Life Committee hopes to capitalize on the stigma that "euthanasia" is presumed to carry by applying the

Cartoon by Mike Smith. Reprinted with permission, **UFS.**

term to a wide range of cases. Some activists insinuate a parallel between the "euthanasia" that includes limits on health care funding and the "euthanasia" that eliminated "life unworthy of life" in Nazi Germany.

Such strategies may backfire. Those who apply the euthanasia label too freely may generate political support for the very practices they oppose. Most Americans still associate euthanasia with compassion and a genuine desire to relieve suffering. In the Kevorkian era these positive associations give euthanasia an aura of moral legitimacy. They are too strong to be dispelled by opponents' attempts to redefine the word or play on fears of Nazi-style genocide. Even physicians and nurses, whose professional codes prohibit participation in euthanasia, often find it hard to reject euthanasia because they associate its aims with values and virtues at the heart of their own practice.

Since euthanasia has become a morally permissible option for increasing numbers of Americans, activists would be wise to recognize that the motives of most supporters are quite different from the crude utilitarianism that is fueling the policies deplored by the National Right to Life Committee.

131

A SIMPLE, BASIC RIGHT

Would assisted suicide save money for HMOs and other greedy health care providers? Probably. Should we keep agonized individuals alive to spite those HMOs? No. Can friends, family members, or doctors exert powerful, selfish influences over an individual's decision? Of course. Yet this happens in every medical decision. We don't deny a woman the right to abortion because she might be pressured into a bad decision; we defend her control over her body, and trust her judgment on what is invariably a wrenching decision....

Geov Parrish. "A Simple, Basic Right." **The Nonviolent Activist.** March/April 1997: 10.

TRUTHFUL TERMS

Those who would deny life-sustaining treatments in order to conserve resources should not be allowed, let alone encouraged, to call the consequences of their proposal "euthanasia." Proponents should be pressed to adopt a more truthful label – such as Battin's "age rationing by denial of treatment."

The importance of such a dialogue extends beyond its relevance to public policy and the common good. Many people experience the anguish reflected in debates on euthanasia and assisted suicide. They use the public discussion of these questions to examine their own stance toward euthanasia or assisted suicide as a possible option for themselves or a loved one. Moreover, the controversy about euthanasia reaches to the very heart of the church's identity. Euthanasia discussions inevitably provoke questions about the meaning and purpose of life and death before God, the nature of our obligations to care for one another and the ethics of a faithful response to suffering.

SYMPATHY TO THE BENEFICIENT MOTIVE

The church should carefully monitor its internal dialogue lest a resource-conserving understanding of euthanasia infiltrate its own language and obscure the real moral challenge of euthanasia: the attractiveness of its compassionate motivation and beneficent intent.

Proponents of euthanasia and assisted suicide deserve a sympathetic if critical hearing both in the church and in the public arena. We should reject a definition of euthanasia that ignores the differences between those motivated by compassion and beneficence and those who would deny life-sustaining treatment for reasons of financial and societal expediency. Any equation of the two positions slanders sincere proponents of euthanasia, and undercuts the possibility of fruitful dialogue about euthanasia and public policy.

READING

20

LEGALITY WILL ENHANCE END-OF-LIFE CARE

Timothy Quill, M.D.

Timothy Quill, M.D., teaches in the Department of Medicine at the University of Rochester. He was one of the petitioners to overturn the assisted suicide ban in the State of New York. The ban was overturned by the Second Circuit Court of Appeals. Upon further challenge by the State of New York, the Supreme Court reversed the Second Circuit Court of Appeals decision June 26, 1997, Vacco v. Quill (138 L.Ed.: 2d 834).

■ POINTS TO CONSIDER

1. According to Quill, has the polarized debate on assisted suicide affected the doctor-patient relationship?

2. Why does the doctor believe physician-assisted suicide should be legal? What methods for voluntary treatment withdrawal test legal boundaries?

3. Describe the narrow interpretation of the Supreme Court's decision for Quill.

4. Summarize the continuity of guidelines for safeguarding the practice of physician-assisted suicide.

Excerpted from the testimony of Timothy Quill, M.D., before the Subcommittee on the Constitution of the U.S. House of Representatives Judiciary Committee, April 29, 1996.

For health care professionals to be more responsive, we will need to be clear about the ethical and legal acceptability of stopping life-sustaining therapy, using high doses of opioid pain relievers, as well as physician-assisted death as a last resort.

The Second Circuit Federal Court unanimously decided that laws arbitrarily prohibiting physician-assisted suicide violate the Equal Protection Clause of the Constitution, thereby reinforcing a similar decision reached by the Ninth Circuit. Viewed narrowly, these decisions will allow suffering, terminally ill patients to openly work with their doctors if they want an assisted death. State legislatures and professional groups have the duty to ensure that such processes are carried out responsibly, but they cannot make access to a physician-assisted death so restricted and difficult that patients have to beg for assistance, or act on their own in despair. In making their decisions, both courts took seriously the heartrending dilemmas faced by dying patients who have no good choices, and see death as their only escape.

A CRY FOR HELP

This decision is a victory for terminally ill patients, but only if other elements of a humane health care system are intact and operational. The decision to seek death should be viewed as a cry for help, the meaning of which can only be determined through careful listening and exploration. Such requests could be the result of undertreated pain or unrecognized depression that might be relieved with good palliative treatment. But these requests might also reflect fully considered, rational wishes to die, in which case the physician's obligations are more complex. Such clinical assessments can be difficult, but are ideally carried out using the collaborative expertise of primary care physicians, and specialists in palliative care and psychiatry.

In the past, if physicians assisted their patients to die by providing lethal prescriptions, they risked prosecution if it was discovered. A recent Washington State survey showed that 16 percent of physicians had received a genuine request for a physician-assisted death within a one year study period, and one quarter of those physicians responded by providing a potentially lethal prescription. Most acted completely in secret, without benefit of consultation. To stay within the law, these physicians would have had to refuse the request even if they agreed that the patient had no other acceptable options, thereby abandoning the patient to act on his own or to continue suffering. Now such processes can potentially be conducted out in the open, collaboratively rather than secretively, subject to carefully constructed safeguards that patients can count on.

BOLSTERING PALLIATIVE CARE

But before we uncritically accept the prospect of legally allowing physician-assisted deaths, we must use this opportunity to ensure that terminally ill patients have full access to hospice care. Hospice care is a highly effective alternative to a "high technology" death in the hospital that many fear. Hospice care costs less and is of higher quality than acute care for the terminally ill, and it is highly effective. It is the standard of care for the dying, against which all other interventions should be measured.

Assisted suicide should never be an alternative to good palliative care. Physician-assisted death should be restricted to those relatively few patients for whom hospice care ceases to be effective, and suffering is so intolerable that death is their only answer. The Second Circuit Court decision acknowledges the devastation experienced by these patients, and considers it a medical emergency which cannot be ignored simply because the public policy challenges are difficult. The patient's personhood is at stake. The interlocked public policy questions include: 1) How can we improve access to good palliative care so that it is available to all terminally ill patients in a timely way? and 2) How should we respond to those infrequent, but troubling patients who still suffer intolerably and want to die in spite of our best efforts?

COMMON GOALS

These court decisions should move the public debate beyond the divisive rhetoric toward consensus building among those with a common interest in improving the care of the dying. It is self-deceptive and demeaning to suggest that all requests for physician-assisted death result from inadequate caring by medical professionals, or from psychopathology or spiritual weakness by patients. Ironically, the chances of having to face these daunting questions may be increased in part because of our successes in helping severely ill patients to live longer with the aid of our vast medical armamentarium. The polarizing discourse and the legal uncertainty in the past have made many physicians even more

136

reluctant than they already were to work closely with their incurably ill and dying patients.

Physicians are already openly involved in some processes that ease death. Patients can stop any life-sustaining treatment, including dialysis, respirators, medicines and fluids, even if it will result in their wished for death. Rapidly increasing doses of opioids can be used to relieve terminal pain, even in amounts that indirectly contribute to a patient's death. (This promise can be very reassuring to a patient who has witnessed a painful death where opioids have been withheld out of ill conceived fears of addiction or of contributing to death.) The primary intent of each of these interventions is to relieve suffering, yet they frequently contribute to the patient's sought after death. Both Circuit Courts have determined that allowing some patients to die simply because they have a life-sustaining treatment to stop or because they have pain that can be aggressively treated discriminates against those who may be suffering more egregiously, but have no such interventions available because of arbitrary elements of their illness. There is a slowly growing consensus within medicine, law and ethics that any treatment that ends life should only be used as a last resort.

SAFEGUARDS

The safeguards proposed by several groups for any physician-assisted death are remarkably similar: 1) The request must come from the patient, who must be mentally competent and fully informed about the alternatives. 2) The patient must be terminally ill, and suffering intolerably in ways that cannot be adequately relieved by palliative measures. 3) An independent second opinion with expertise in palliative medicine must verify that the patient meets agreed-upon criteria. A psychiatrist should evaluate the patient if there are questions about mental capacity. 4) Explicit processes of documentation, reporting, and review should be in place so the practice can be better understood, improved over time, and monitored. The courts have now challenged the states and professionals under their jurisdiction to operationalize such safeguards into a system that is responsive to and protective of terminally ill patients.

BAD DEATH AS MEDICAL EMERGENCY

In the current unstable medical and legal climates, we must teach doctors and reassure patients that the medical profession will fulfill its obligation to maintain continuity of care using skilled palliative methods with their dying patients, and respond to the few remaining bad deaths as medical emergencies. For health care professionals to be more responsive, we will need to be clear about the ethical and legal acceptability of stopping life-sustaining therapy, using high doses of opioid pain relievers, as well as physician-assisted death as a last resort. Instead of pretending that we do not currently ease death, we must now work together to develop clinical, ethical, and legal guidelines, and then carefully research whether they are acceptable to patients and effective at preventing abuse. All available options to alleviate suffering must be publicized to both physicians and patients, for we have an obligation to be responsive to those who are disintegrating as persons in spite of our best efforts without violating their or our personal values. The method used to help patients at the very end is less important than more fundamental processes of caring, joint decision making, excellent palliative care, and a commitment not to abandon no matter how the process unfolds. The recent Circuit Court decisions reinforce this commitment, and bring it out in the open instead of behind closed doors.

PHYSICIAN-ASSISTED SUICIDE CONTRADICTS DOCTORS' MISSION

Lonnie R. Bristow, M.D.

Lonnie R. Bristow, M.D., practices internal medicine in San Pablo, California. He also serves as the president of the American Medical Association (AMA). The AMA is the largest professional association of American physicians.

■ POINTS TO CONSIDER

1. What is the principle of double effect?

2. Evaluate the distinction Bristow makes between withdrawing treatment and prescribing medications to hasten death.

3. What claims does the author make concerning physician-assisted suicide and its effect on the doctor-patient relationship?

4. Discuss the author's view on pain management and its place in the physician-assisted suicide discourse.

Excerpted from the testimony of Lonnie R. Bristow, M.D., before the Subcommittee on the Constitution of the U.S. House of Representatives Judiciary Committee, April 29, 1996.

The movement for legally sanctioning physician-assisted suicide is a sign of society's failure to address the complex issues raised at the end of life. It is not a victory for personal rights.

For nearly 2,500 years, physicians have vowed to "give no deadly drug if asked for it, nor make a suggestion to this effect." What has changed, that there should be this attempt to make "assisted suicide" an accepted practice of medicine? Certainly the experience of physical pain has not changed over time. Yet the blessings of medical research and technology present their own new challenges, as our ability to delay or draw out the dying process alters our perceptions and needs.

INCONSISTENT

The American Medical Association (AMA) believes that physician-assisted suicide is unethical and fundamentally inconsistent with the pledge physicians make to devote themselves to healing and to life. Laws that sanction physician-assisted suicide undermine the foundation of the patient-physician relationship that is grounded in the patient's trust that the physician is working wholeheartedly for the patient's health and welfare. The multidisciplinary members of the New York State Task Force on Life and the Law concur in this belief, writing that "physician-assisted suicide and euthanasia violate values that are fundamental to the practice of medicine and the patient-physician relationship."

Yet physicians also have an ethical responsibility to relieve pain and to respect their patient's wishes regarding care, and it is when these duties converge at the bedside of a seriously or terminally ill patient that physicians are torn.

OBLIGATIONS

The AMA believes that these additional ethical duties require physicians to respond aggressively to the needs of the patients at the end of life with adequate pain control, emotional support, comfort care, respect for patient autonomy and good communications.

Further efforts are necessary to better educate physicians in the areas of pain management and effective end-of-life care. Patient education is the other essential component of an effective outreach to minimize the circumstances which might lead to a patient's request for physician-assisted suicide: inadequate social support; the perceived burden to family and friends; clinical depression; hopelessness; loss of self-esteem; and the fear of living with chronic, unrelieved pain.

Patients who believe sudden and "controlled" death would protect them from the perceived indignities of prolonged deterioration and terminal illness must receive social support as well as the support of the profession to work through these issues. Providing assisted suicide would breach the ethical means of medicine to safeguard patients' dignity and independence.

PAIN MANAGEMENT

Many proponents of assisted suicide cite a fear of prolonged suffering and unmanageable pain as support for their position. For most patients, advancements in palliative care can adequately control pain through oral medications, nerve blocks or radiotherapy. We all recognize, however, that there are patients whose intractable pain cannot be relieved by treating the area, organ or system perceived as the source of the pain. For patients for whom pain cannot be controlled by other means, it is ethically permissible for physicians to administer sufficient levels of controlled substances to ease pain, even if the patient's risk of addiction or death is increased.

The failure of most states to expressly permit this practice has generated reluctance among physicians to prescribe adequate pain medication. Additional uncertainty is produced by the potential for legal action against the physician when controlled substances are prescribed in large amounts to treat patients with intractable pain. This uncertainty chills physicians' ability to effectively control their terminally ill patients' pain and suffering through the appropriate prescription and administration of opiates and other controlled substances.

DOUBLE EFFECT

In some instances, administration of adequate pain medication will have the secondary effect of suppressing the respiration of the patient, thereby hastening death. This is commonly referred to as the "double effect." The distinction between this action and assisted suicide is crucial. The physician has an obligation to provide for the comfort of the patient. If there are no alternatives but to

141

Cartoon by Richard Wright.

increase the risk of death in order to provide that comfort, the physician is ethically permitted to exercise that option. In this circumstance, the physician's clinical decision is guided by the intent to provide pain relief, rather than the intent to cause death. This distinguishes the ethical use of palliative care medications from the unethical application of medical skills to cause death.

MORAL DISTINCTIONS

Some participants in the debate about assisted suicide see no meaningful distinction between withholding or withdrawing treatment and providing assistance in suicide. They argue that the results of each action are the same and therefore the acts themselves carry equal moral status. This argument largely ignores the distinction between act and omission in the circumstances of terminal care and does not address many of the principles that underlie the right of patients to refuse the continuation of medical care and the duty of physicians to exercise their best clinical judgment.

Specifically, proponents who voice this line of reasoning fail to recognize the crucial difference between a patient's right to refuse unwanted medical treatment and any proposed right to receive medical intervention which would cause death. Withholding or withdrawing treatment allows death to proceed naturally, with the underlying disease being the cause of death. Assisted suicide, on the other hand, requires action to cause death, independent from the disease process.

THE "SLIPPERY SLOPE"

Physician-assisted suicide raises troubling and unsurmountable "slippery slope" problems. Despite attempts by some, it is difficult to imagine adequate safeguards which could effectively guarantee that patients' decisions to request assisted suicide were unambivalent, informed and free of coercion.

A policy allowing assisted suicide could also result in the victimization of poor and disenfranchised populations who may have greater financial burdens and social burdens which could be

143

"relieved" by hastening death. As reported by the New York State Task Force on Life and the Law (composed of bioethicists, lawyers, clergy and state health officials), "assisted suicide and euthanasia will be practiced through the prism of social inequality and prejudice that characterizes the delivery of services in all segments of society, including health care."

Recent studies documenting reasons for patient requests for physician-assisted suicide speak to our "slippery slope" concerns. Patients were rarely suffering intractable pain. Rather, they cited fears of losing control, being a burden, being dependent on others for personal care and loss of dignity often associated with end-stage disease.

HOLLOW VICTORIES

The movement for legally sanctioning physician-assisted suicide is a sign of society's failure to address the complex issues raised at the end of life. It is not a victory for personal rights. We are equipped with the tools to effectively manage end-of-life pain and to offer terminally ill patients dignity and to add value to their remaining time. As the voice of the medical profession, the AMA offers its capability to coordinate multidisciplinary discourse on end-of-life issues, for it is essential to coordinate medical educators, patients, advocacy organizations, allied health professionals and the counseling and pastoral professions to reach a comprehensive solution to these challenging issues. Our response should be a better informed medical profession and public, working together to preserve fundamental values at the end of life.

IN MY OPINION

This activity may be used as an individualized study guide for students in libraries and resource centers or as a discussion catalyst in small group and classroom discussions.

Guidlines

Examine your own thoughts and feelings about the issue of physician-assisted suicide. Read through the following statements and evaluate each one as indicated. Be prepared to discuss your evaluations in a general class discussion.

Mark (A) for statements with which you agree.
Mark (D) for statements with which you disagree.
Mark (O) for statements about which you are not sure.
Mark (X) for statements which reflect themes from any of the readings in the book.

_____1. Euthanasia should be legal.

_____2. Life begins at conception.

_____3. Dependence at the end of life should not be viewed as undignified.

_____4. The pain of a tiny fraction of the dying population does not justify a change in the law with regard to euthanasia.

_____5. Life begins at birth.

_____6. Physician-assisted suicide should be illegal.

_____7. Physicians need to pursue care that is consistent with the patient's wishes.

_____8. Hospice is the only ethical means to treat the terminally ill, in pain.

_____9. Hospice is one viable option, among many including physician-assisted suicide, for end-of-life care.

_____10. For-profit health care and physician-assisted suicide are a dangerous mix.

_____11. The physical and emotional state of an individual before death affects a loved one's image of the individual.

_____12. Physician-assisted suicide, like militarism, the death penalty and abortion, destroys the seamless web of life.

_____13. My body, like my thoughts, is autonomous. No ruling of law should intefere with decisions I make with my body.

_____14. It is unethical for doctors to partake in killing.

_____15. Physician-assisted suicide should be legal.

_____16. Outside and internal pressure inevitably affect decisions. This must never be an excuse for denying individuals the right to make his/her own decisions.

_____17. Everyone must pay more attention to the care of the dying.

_____18. Polarized issues like physician-assisted suicide consume a disproportionate amount of the national debate.

_____19. The experience in the twentieth century makes it clear that doctor-assisted suicide and euthanasia should remain part of the past.

BIBLIOGRAPHY

Book References

Active Euthanasia, Religion, and the Public Debate. Chicago: Park Ridge Center, 1991.

Adams, Judith A. **The Living Will or Death with Dignity: Legislation and Issues.** Washington, DC: Georgetown University, Joseph and Rose Kennedy Institute of Ethics, 1984.

American Association of Suicidology. **Report of the Committee on Physician-Assisted Suicide and Euthanasia.** New York: Guilford Press, 1996.

Battin, M. Pabst, et al. **Physician-Assisted Suicide: Expanding the Debate.** New York: Routledge, 1998.

Burleigh, Michael. **Confronting the Nazi Past: New Debates on Modern German History.** New York: St. Martin's Press, 1996.

Burleigh, Michael. **Death and Deliverance: "Euthanasia" in Germany c. 1900-1945.** New York: Cambridge University Press, 1994.

Burleigh, Michael. **Ethics and Extermination: Reflections on Nazi Genocide.** New York: Cambridge University Press, 1997.

Burnell, George M. **Final Choices: To Live or to Die in an Age of Medical Technology.** New York: Insight Books, 1993.

Caplan, Arthur L. **Moral Matters: Ethical Issues in Medicine and the Life Sciences.** New York: Wiley, 1995.

Carrick, Paul. **Medical Ethics in Antiquity: Philosophical Perspectives on Abortion and Euthanasia.** Boston: Kluwer Academic Publishers, 1985.

Clark, Nina. **The Politics of Physician-Assisted Suicide.** New York: Garland, 1997.

Cox, Donald W. **Hemlock's Cup: The Struggle for Death with Dignity.** Buffalo, NY: Prometheus Books, 1993.

Cundiff, David. **Euthanasia Is Not the Answer: A Hospice Physician's View.** Totowa, NJ: Humana Press, 1992.

DeSimone, Cathleen. **Death on Demand: Physician-Assisted Suicide in the United States.** Buffalo, NY: W.S. Hein, 1996.

Dworkin, Gerald, et al. **Euthanasia and Physician-Assisted Suicide.** New York: Cambridge University Press, 1998.

Emanuel, Linda L. **Regulating How We Die: The Ethical, Medical, and Legal Issues Surrounding Physician-Assisted Suicide.** Cambridge, MA: Harvard University Press, 1998.

Grubb, Andrew. **Choices and Decisions in Health Care.** Chichester, NY: Wiley, 1993.

Humber, James M., et al. **Physician-Assisted Death.** Totowa, N.J.: Humana Press, 1994.

Keown, John. **Euthanasia Examined: Ethical, Clinical, and Legal Perspectives.** New York: Cambridge University Press, 1997.

McKhann, Charles F. **A Time to Die: The Place for Physician Assistance.** New Haven, CT: Yale University Press, 1999.

McLean, Sheila A.M. and Alison Britton. **The Case for Physician-Assisted Suicide.** London: Pandora, 1997.

Moreno, Jonathan D. **Arguing Euthanasia: The Controversy Over Mercy Killing, Assisted Suicide, and the "Right to Die."** New York: Simon & Schuster, 1995.

Walters, James W. **Choosing Who's to Live: Ethics and Aging.** Urbana: University of Illinois Press, 1996.

Weir, Robert F. **Physician-Assisted Suicide.** Bloomington: Indiana University Press, 1997.

Wildes, Kevin W. and Alan C. Mitchell. **Choosing Life: A Dialogue on Evangelum Vitae.** Washington, DC: Georgetown University Press, 1997.

Journal References:

Ackerman, Felicia. "Goldilocks and Mrs. Ilych: A Critical Look at the 'Philosophy of Hospice'." **Cambridge Quarterly of Healthcare Ethics.** Summer 1997.

Admiraal, Pieter V. "Euthanasia in the Netherlands." **Free Inquiry.** Winter 1996-7.

American Medical Association, Council on Scientific Affairs. "Good Care of the Dying Patient [council report]." **Journal of the American Medical Association.** February 14, 1996.

Arras, John D. "Physician-Assisted Suicide: A Tragic View." **Journal of Contemporary Health Law and Policy.** Spring 1997.

Birchard, Karen. "Many Irish Doctors in Favour of Physician-Assisted Suicide." **The Lancet.** September 6, 1997.

Brodie, Keith H. and Leslie Banner. "Normatology: A Review and Commentary with Reference to Abortion and Physician-Assisted Suicide." **American Journal of Psychiatry.** June 1997.

Brody, Howard, and Gregg K. Vanderkieft. "Physician-Assisted Suicide: A Very Personal Issue." **American Family Physician.** May 15, 1997.

Brown, Gary. "A Cure Worse Than the Disease." **America.** December 14-21, 1996.

Butler, Robert N. "The Dangers of Physician-Assisted Suicide: Will We Choose to Provide a Right to Euthanasia for the Few or Palliative Care for the Many?" **Geriatrics.** July 1996.

Churchill, Larry R. and Nancy King. "Physician-Assisted Suicide, Euthanasia, or Withdrawal of Treatment: Distinguishing Between Them Clarifies Moral, Legal, and Practical Positions. **British Medical Journal.** July 19, 1997.

Conlan, Michael F. "Pharmacists Share Divergent Views on Assisted Suicide." **Drug Topics.** February 3, 1997.

"Death and Dignity: Physician-Assisted Suicide." **The Nation.** February 3, 1997.

148

Deftos, Leonard J., M.D., "Physician Assistance in Dying." **Post-Graduate Medicine.** June 1997.

Dority, Barbara. "Physician Aid-in-Dying: Within Some of Our Lifetimes?" **The Humanist.** September 19, 1997.

Duffy, Tom and Timothy Quill. "In the Name of Mercy: The Anti-Kevorkian Dr. Timothy Quill Makes His Case for Assisted Suicide." **People.** April 7, 1997.

Dylan Lowe, Alexandra. "Facing the Final Exit." **American Bar Association Journal.** September 1997.

Emanuel, Ezekial. "Whose Right to Die? America Should Think Again Before Pressing Ahead with the Legalization of Physician-Assisted Suicide and Voluntary Euthanasia." **The Atlantic Monthly.** March 1997.

"Fatal Prescription: Re-enactment of the Oregon Death with Dignity Act on Physician-Assisted Suicide." **Commonweal.** December 1997.

"A French Debate about Death." **The Economist.** August 15, 1998.

Ganzini, Linda and Melinda A. Lee. "Psychiatry and Assisted Suicide in the United States." **The New England Journal of Medicine.** June 19, 1997.

Gates, Thomas J. "Euthanasia and Assisted Suicide: A Family Practice Perspective." **American Family Physician.** May 15, 1997.

"The Goals of Medicine: Setting New Priorities." **The Hastings Center Report.** November/December 1996.

Groenewoud, Johanna H., et al. "Physician-Assisted Death in Psychiatric Practice in the Netherlands." **The New England Journal of Medicine.** June 19, 1997.

Hall, Charles E. and Cecil McIver. "No Longer an Option for One AIDS Patient and His Doctor: Physician-Assisted Suicide. **Medical Economics.** September 8, 1997.

Hardwig, John. "Is There a Duty to Die?" **The Hastings Center Report.** March 13, 1997.

Hendin, Herbert. "Physician-Assisted Suicide: A Look at the Netherlands." **Current.** December 1997.

Hopkins, Patrick D. "Why Does Removing Machines Count as 'Passive' Euthanasia?" **The Hastings Center Report.** May/June 1997.

Hyary, Heta. "Bioethics and Political Ideology: The Case of Active Voluntary Euthanasia." **Bioethics.** July/October 1997.

"Is There a Right to Die?" **The Christian Century.** January 22, 1997.

Jaklevic, Mary Chris. "The Hidden Debate: Providers Fear Impact of Regulations on Assisted Suicide. **Modern Healthcare.** February 17, 1997.

Keenan, James F. "The Case for Physician-Assisted Suicide?" **America.** November 14, 1998.

Klotzko, Arlene Judith. "What Kind of Life? What Kind of Death? An Interview with Dr. Henk Prins." **Bioethics.** January 1997.

Koch, Tom. "Living Versus Dying 'with Dignity': A New Perspective on the Euthanasia Debate." **Cambridge Quarterly of Healthcare Ethics.** Winter 1996.

Kowalski, Susan D. "Assisted Suicide: Is There a Future?" **Critical Care Nursing Quarterly.** May 1996.

May, Barbara, et al. "Life-Terminating Choices: A Framework for Nursing Decision Making." **Nursing and Health Care Perspectives.** July 17, 1997.

Meisel, Alan. "The 'Right to Die': A Case Study in American Lawmaking." **European Journal of Health and Law.** March 1996.

Paris, John J. "Autonomy and Physician-Assisted Suicide." **America.** May 17, 1997.

Peck, Richard L. "End-of-Life Decisionmaking Takes Center Stage." **Nursing Homes.** March 1997.

Post, Stephen G. "Physician-Assisted Suicide in Alzheimer's Disease." **Journal of the American Geriatrics Society.** May 1997.

Pullicino, Patrick, et al. "Physician-Assisted Suicide." **Annals of Internal Medicine.** July 15, 1997.

Quinn, Kevin P. "Assisted Suicide and Equal Protection: In Defense of the Distinction between Killing and Letting Die." **Issues in Law and Medicine.** September 22, 1997.

Safranek, John P. "Autonomy and Assisted Suicide: The Execution of Freedom." **The Hastings Center Report.** July 1, 1998.

Shapiro, Joseph P. "Euthanasia's Home: What the Dutch Experience Can Teach Americans about Assisted Suicide." **U.S. News and World Report.** January 13, 1997.

Sharpe, Virginia A. and Edmund D. Pellegrino. "Medical Ethics in the Courtroom: A Reappraisal." **Journal of Medicine and Philosophy.** August 1997.

Sullivan, Mark D., et al. "Should Psychiatrists Serve as Gatekeepers for Physician-Assisted Suicide?" **The Hastings Center Report.** July 1, 1998.

"Survey of Approval of Australia's Northern Territory Rights of the Terminally Ill Act." **The Lancet.** February 22, 1997.

Valente, Sharon M. and Donna Trainor. "Rational Suicide among Patients Who Are Terminally Ill." **AORN Journal.** August 1998.

van der Heide, Agnes, et al. "Medical End-of-Life Decisions Made for Neonates and Infants in the Netherlands." **The Lancet.** July 26, 1997.

van der Maas, Paul J. "End of Life Decisions in Mentally Disabled People: Protecting Vulnerable Life Does Not Mean Prolonging It Regardless of Suffering." **British Medical Journal.** July 12, 1997.

Victor, Kirk. "Bashing the Bench." **The National Journal.** May 31, 1997.

INDEX